Praise for *Point Well Made*

"*Point Well Made* is a remarkable resource for every courtroom advocate presenting arguments to the bench. It offers tremendous practical advice, addressing challenges lawyers frequently encounter and offering specific tips and language choices. How I wish every attorney would study this volume before entering my courtroom."

> — Hon. Patricia M. Lucas, Presiding Judge of California Superior Court, Santa Clara County

"*Point Well Made* offers a blueprint for how to prepare for motion argument complete with useful tools and clear examples. Judge Vaidik and Rebecca Diaz-Bonilla demystify the process of preparing to argue a motion, and they offer specific preparation advice and delivery tips to ensure that you will be able to execute in court. The book also lays out the concerns that motivate judges and offers tips for how to address them, as well as advice for how to assess and approach judges with different work styles, personalities, and beliefs. It even tackles what many lawyers view as the toughest part of the argument—responding to questions—with a foolproof, six-point process. *Point Well Made* should be required reading for litigators."

> — Mariana Hogan, Professor of Law and Director of Advocacy Programs, New York Law School

"It's been my privilege and my pleasure to teach with both Chief Judge Vaidik and Ms. Diaz-Bonilla at various NITA programs. Whenever I do, I always come away with something of lasting value. This book provides a wealth of ideas, techniques, and processes that cannot fail to make everyone who reads it a better, more effective advocate. And as a sitting judge, I hope that the lawyers who appear in front of me read this book cover to cover!"

> — Hon. Robert L. McGahey, Jr., District Judge, Second Judicial District, Denver

"Arguing motions seems easy enough. It isn't. In a practical yet comprehensive guide to effectively arguing motions, Judge Nancy Vaidik and her public-speaking trainer and lawyer colleague Rebecca Diaz-Bonilla have written a first-rate guide to persuasive motion practice. Every lawyer who argues motions should read this book."

> — Michael J. Dale, Professor of Law, Nova Southeastern University Shepard Broad College of Law

"*Point Well Made* is a well-written, thorough examination of all of the aspects of motion practice, including nuances of preparation and style seldom contemplated by the more casual commentator. Judge Vaidik and Ms. Diaz-Bonilla have done us a favor. They have inspired lawyers to think beyond simply the technical and mundane aspects of motion advocacy and focused on the heart of persuasion. Anyone who reads this book, whether a lawyer or a public speaker of any kind, will be enriched by its lessons in advocacy."

> — Hon. Lorna Propes, Circuit Court of Cook County, Illinois

POINT WELL MADE

ORAL ADVOCACY IN MOTION PRACTICE

POINT WELL MADE

ORAL ADVOCACY IN MOTION PRACTICE

Hon. Nancy Harris Vaidik
Indiana Court of Appeals

Rebecca Diaz-Bonilla
Lumen8 Advisors, LLC

NATIONAL INSTITUTE FOR TRIAL ADVOCACY

Address inquiries to:

Reprint Permission
National Institute for Trial Advocacy
1685 38th Street, Suite 200
Boulder, CO 80301-2735
Phone: (800) 225-6482
Fax: (720) 890-7069
Email: permissions@nita.org

ISBN 978-1-60156-621-8
eISBN 978-1-60156-622-5

FBA 1621

Library of Congress Cataloging-in-Publication Data

Names: Vaidik, Nancy, author. | Diaz-Bonilla, Rebecca, author.

Title: Point well made: oral advocacy in motion practice / Nancy Harris Vaidik, Indiana Court of Appeals; Rebecca Diaz-Bonilla, Lumen8 Advisors, LLC.

Description: Boulder, CO: National Institute for Trial Advocacy, [2016] | Includes index.

Identifiers: LCCN 2016043799 | ISBN 9781601566218

Subjects: LCSH: Oral pleading--United States. | Trial practice--United States. | Appellate procedure--United States. | LCGFT: Trial and arbitral proceedings.

Classification: LCC KF8915 .V35 2016 | DDC 347.73/72--dc23 LC record available at https://lccn.loc.gov/2016043799

Printed in the United States.

Cover design concept by Julie McDonald.

 Wolters Kluwer

Official co-publisher of NITA.
WKLegaledu.com/NITA

Acknowledgements

A special thanks to Beth Sher, Bob Stein, and Mariah Brandt, all extraordinary lawyers, who shared their thoughts about motion practice with us. Also, a huge thank you to our editor, Marsi Buckmelter.

CONTENTS

Chapter Three: Themes: The *What*, the *Why*, and the *How*

Chapter Four: Facts

Chapter Five: The Law

Chapter Six: Responding to Questions

Chapter Seven: Structure and Preparation Systems

Chapter Eight: Rebuttals

PREFACE

A young woman enters a chess championship. Among other factors, her preparation depends on her experience level, the skills of her opponent, the importance of the competition, and imposed time constraints. She may be so experienced that she need only review her opening moves, briefly research her opponent, and get a good night's sleep. Likewise, planning for your next motion hearing depends on your experience, the opponent, the complexity of your motion, the time allotted by the court, and the stakes involved. Nevertheless, all good advocates, whether seasoned at motion hearings or not, must spend some time planning and practicing.

The frequency and complexity of your motion practice may vary, but the core components of how to think about and prepare for a motion hearing are the same. If you are a prosecutor handling several motions every day before a familiar judge, your preparation will be quite different than for the intellectual property litigator preparing for a *Markman* hearing in Washington, D.C. Sometimes you will prepare with little time, but other times you will have months to practice.

After the motion, response, and reply are written, how do you persuade a judge, magistrate, or arbitrator to see it your way in a limited amount of time? Most attorneys are well trained at writing. They fine-tune the craft and become skilled at persuading through the papers of a motion. But a ruling in your favor can often be the result of successful advocacy. Being ready to persuasively answer questions like, "Why are we here, counselor?" could determine the success or failure of this chapter of your case. This book reveals the tools of success, tried and true.

This is not a book about when or how to file or respond to certain motions. This is not a book about how to draft pleadings and motions. This is not a book about litigation strategy. This is not a book about how to prepare and call witnesses. *Point Well Made* is a book about how to spark a fruitful discussion with the court during a motion hearing. A properly argued motion affords you the chance to discover what matters to the judge and, hopefully, for him to find a way to rule in your favor.

Great oral advocacy in motion practice rarely happens naturally. It takes confidence, logic, and likability to convince the court. The attorney must possess a natural ability to excel in prepared and spontaneous rhetoric styles, or learn the skills necessary to achieve those skills. This book focuses on both genres, prepared and spontaneous. These skills sets require development and practice. This book provides best practices and trusted secrets of success. Just like any best practice in writing, sports, or music competitions, an attorney should first master the rules and then know how and when to break those rules. Breaking the rules requires a keen self-awareness and an instant read on the moment at hand. A great litigator in motion practice stays flexible. She relies on the prepared material, but abandons the game plan when the circumstances demand. She shifts when needed to successfully persuade.

Each advocate brings her own education, experience, talents, fears, physicality, voice, and personality to the motion hearing. These factors influence which recommendations are always followed, sometimes followed, and never followed for each individual.

The book is co-authored to bring you two perspectives. Judge Nancy Harris Vaidik is the Chief Judge of the Indiana Court of Appeals. As a prosecutor and a private practitioner, she argued hundreds of motions. She served as a trial court judge for eight years before being appointed to the Indiana Court of Appeals, serving for over fifteen years. Judge Vaidik has been an adjunct professor of law at Indiana University Maurer School of Law for the past fifteen years, teaching trial advocacy. She developed the motion training program for the National Institute for Trial Advocacy (NITA), and teaches internationally.

Rebecca Diaz-Bonilla is an international communications consultant and an attorney. She has coached litigators for over a decade in motion practice. Mrs. Diaz-Bonilla systemized motions preparation for clients, bringing her experience in developing substance, voice, and body language for advocates of all levels. She was an adjunct professor at University of Virginia School of Law, and now serves as a communications faculty member for NITA. She authored the award-winning book, *Foolproof: An Attorney's Guide to Communication.*

CHAPTER ONE

PREPARING FOR THE HEARING

Your heart races, brain fogs, hands shake, and stomach turns. You stammer: "Uh, I'm not certain, Your Honor. I mean, I wish I had thought of that . . . ."

The judge interrupts: "This case was cited several times in your brief, counselor. Am I remembering that correctly?"

"Oh, um, no, I mean, yes, Your Honor. My associate researched that case, and I knew the facts, I mean, um, I thought . . . ."

"Why are you wasting my time today? Isn't this your motion?" questions the judge.

Trainwreck. Take two.

Your heart races, brain fogs, hands shake, and stomach turns. "If Your Honor could give me a moment, I will review those facts." (Ten-second pause as you consult your notes.)

"This case was cited several times in your brief, counselor. Am I remembering that correctly?" asks the judge.

You calmly reply, "Yes, Your Honor. You have that correct. The facts in *Smith v. Texas* are indeed close to the dispute before Your Honor today. Procedurally, the trial court in *Smith* disagreed with the government, but the Department of Labor won on appeal. Those facts are similar to ours. A Freedom of Information Act (FOIA) request must be narrow in scope. Here, the citizen wants records spanning 120 years."

The judge nods. You transition and sense success.

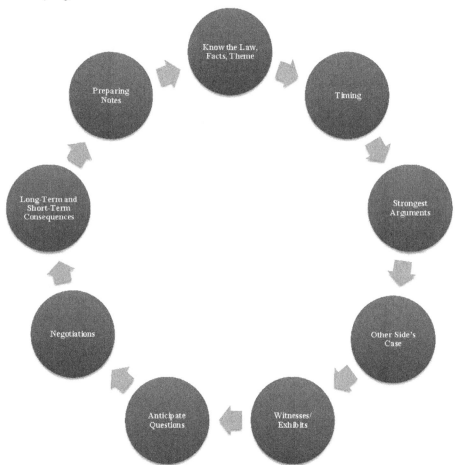

Successful planning for a motion hearing involves preparing for spontaneity. It may well be you deliver an uninterrupted monologue that you have carefully prepared in advance of the hearing. A more likely scenario, and the one that is ultimately better for your client, is that you engage in a dialogue with the judge—one that you may or may not have *precisely* anticipated, but one you anticipated nonetheless. A successful presentation is a prepared, yet spontaneous, delivery from a credible attorney who quickly gets to the point and has anticipated and prepared for possible trainwrecks.

Preparing for a motion hearing is similar to what a high school senior goes through as she gears up to talk to her parents about her college options. Our senior has been accepted into three different colleges—a private college, a state university, and a community college—and has decided that the private college is the best choice. Naturally, she needs her parents' consent and support, and knows that to be persuasive, she must lay some groundwork before she even approaches them. She needs *facts*. How much is tuition at each school? What programs and majors have the best reputation, and do they align with her career interests? What is their job placement rate for graduates? With these facts at her fingertips, our senior can then craft two or three of her best arguments in favor of private college.

She is no dummy though: she has also thought through the weaknesses of her arguments, for surely her parents will press her about them. For example, a private college is expensive. Is financial aid available? How likely is she to qualify for it? What about scholarships? She is smart enough to know that her parents will make points that she will have to concede. There is no getting around the fact that there is an enormous cost differential between community college and private college tuition—and she knows that if she hopes to maintain her credibility, she must concede that point. But our plucky senior has also considered the long-term and short-term consequences of choosing the private college. In the short run, yes, community college is cheaper, but in the long run, being a graduate of a top-flight private college would likely result in a higher lifelong income that, over time, would offset its pricier tuition.

Last, she must contemplate her fallback position, her Plan B in the event her parents insist that private school is not a viable option. Is she willing to go to the mat over it—or will she agree to meet her parents in the middle and go with the state school as her second choice? She has a clear preference, and an even clearer idea of what option she wants to reject.

Planning for a motion hearing requires the same considerations, but with added risk and tension. In a motion hearing, you are fighting for the outcome of someone else. You must know the facts and the law, create a theme that explains why you win and why the court should care, identify your two or three strongest arguments, pinpoint your Achilles' heel, anticipate questions and potential concessions, recognize the long-term and short-term consequences of the motion, and contemplate a fallback position.

1.1   Know the Legal Theory and Its Support

Before the hearing, review the legal theory supporting your motion. The legal theory addresses what must be legally proven or disproven, including the legal elements, cases, rules, and statutes upholding your position. Undoubtedly, you decided on a theory before you filed the motion and its accompanying papers.

Review your legal theory and the law cited in your briefs, making yourself comfortable with those crucial three or four cases your motion turns on. Be able to show why the facts of these three or four cases are similar to or different than yours.

The judge does not want you to read the entire case to her. She wants a concise and relevant understanding of the case law, statutes, or regulations that govern the legal theories presented. You need to be able to discuss the law, not just report it.

The day before the hearing, check the cases upon which you rely to ensure that none of them have been refined or overruled.

1.1.1 Magic Words

A dialogue with the judge about the law is easier to understand if you concentrate on the magic words of the case. Key phrases like "excusable neglect," "likelihood of success on the merits," and "reason to believe that criminal activity is afoot" can be the foundation of a successful argument. A good start to preparing the law of the motion is to learn the key words and phrases of the supporting law. These are not full sentences. Practice them aloud, again and yet again. They must glide off your lips without hesitation.

Key words allow you to find the universal language of the motion. Rarely is the motion the first one of its type heard by the court. If you appropriately use this familiar language, judges do not need to work hard to understand your legal arguments and can categorize your case into the appropriate legal box. In the absence of those well-known phrases, however, you run the risk of complicating the law, making it more difficult for the judge to understand your points and rule in your favor.

Sometimes, the motion is unusual and the law is unknown to the court. In that case, there is no common phraseology known to the court. Nevertheless, find the critical language of the cases on which you are relying. To make the legal issues understandable for the court, pluck simple phrases from the case and use them to your advantage. Not only will this preparation make it more likely that your arguments will be clear and understandable, but upon reading the cases cited, the judge or clerk should hear your words reverberate in her mind, enhancing your credibility.

1.1.2 Understanding the Rationale Behind the Law

Investigate and identify the rationale or public policy behind the law. Ask yourself why the law is written as it is. Knowing the reasons behind the law allows you to develop common-sense arguments supporting your position.

Suppose in a motion in limine hearing your opponent asks that certain business records be excluded from evidence as hearsay. Of course, you will argue for their admission under Federal Rule of Evidence 803(6), but it is even more compelling and persuasive if you also argue the *reasons* these records are deemed trustworthy. Show the judge why and how the business operates with the records and how the records are important to the operation.

Similarly, if you represent the petitioner in a preliminary injunction hearing to protect a trade secret from being used by the respondent, you are likely to succeed on the merits in the underlying action if you argue that the legal elements of a trade secret are met. To be even more convincing, argue that the very purpose of protecting a trade secret is to incentivize innovation, a purpose undermined by denying injunctive relief and allowing the respondent access to the trade secret.

Identifying the purpose or policy reasons behind the law provides a source for convincing, persuasive, common sense arguments—with the added bonus that these common sense arguments are simple and easily comprehended by a judge with a full docket.

Closely aligned with knowing the rationale behind the law is understanding the development of the law. A law's evolution informs its current status and future trend. Read the key cases chronologically to identify trends. Predict the natural future progression of the law based upon its history. For cases in which the law is not yet on your side but the equities are, this approach may provide your best argument.

1.1.3   *Knowing the Law = Credibility*

Credibility depends in large part on your knowledge of the issue before the court. When the judge looks for an answer, you want to be the go-to person on whom the court relies. You may serve that role only if you are prepared with a full and complete understanding of your case. A judge will detect your level of understanding based on your grasp of the legal theory. You cannot hide. A judge knows when you are pretending. As you prepare, it is essential to learn and fully understand the law.

Most motions are only one piece of the puzzle. Chances are, you will be back before this judge—if not on this case, then another. To avoid the temptation of exaggerating your knowledge of the law to a judge, do your homework. The goal should be to preserve the trust between you and the judge at all times. Think: long-term relationships over one-time transactions.

1.2   Review and Refine Your Factual Theory

A thorough understanding of the facts also establishes and maintains your credibility. Prepare to be credible by knowing the facts underlying your motion. Although knowledge of both the facts and the law are important, seasoned advocates argue that knowledge of the *facts* is more important. Judges have little trouble finding the law of the case—and, in many respects, are experts in the law. Regarding the facts of your case, you are the expert. Judges rely on your expertise of the facts. The key facts, both good and bad, should be at your fingertips during the hearing. Relevant quotes from documents should be in your motion portfolio so there is no fumbling during your discussion with the court.

Before the hearing, review and refine your factual theory. The factual theory is why the composite of your facts results in you *winning your motion*. Know the good facts that support your theory, the neutral facts that neither support nor harm you, and the bad facts that hurt your position.

The facts may be relatively few, as in a motion to dismiss for failure to state a claim upon which relief can be granted. Because a motion to dismiss tests only the legal sufficiency of the pleading and not the facts supporting it, the facts are limited. On the other hand, a summary judgment motion or a motion for injunctive relief may involve many facts from many sources, including those from depositions and affidavits.

For fact-intensive motions or those with complicated law, many attorneys engage in brainstorming sessions before both writing and arguing the motion. With a whiteboard, an hour's time, and possibly a colleague:

- Write the legal elements of the motion.

- List the facts, in a non-judgmental way, as being good, bad, or neutral to the case, by placing good facts in one column, bad facts in another, and neutral facts in both columns. Be sure to list only facts, and not conclusions.

- Identify the three best facts and three worst facts.

Eventually, a factual theory develops that explains what happened, why it happened, and why you should win. The factual theory must explain your good and bad facts, be believable and simple, and address your legal elements.

Consider this example. You represent Sam Smith in a bad faith claim against Acme Insurance Company, Inc. Sam sustained injuries in a car accident. The tortfeasor's insurance company paid its policy limits to Sam. Sam was insured by Acme Insurance Company. His policy provided underinsured motorist coverage with limits of $50,000. After investigating the claim, Acme refused to pay any money to Sam. You filed a breach of contract claim against Acme, which you won. Weeks later, you filed a complaint on Sam's behalf against Acme for breach of its implied covenant of good faith and fair dealing.

You file your lawsuit on January 10. On March 1, you served a request for production of documents demanding a copy of all complaints filed in any court against Acme by its insureds for bad faith claims arising out of underinsured motorist coverage. You also requested a copy of all claim forms filed, depositions taken, or affidavits of adjustors, supervisors, or company officers filed in those suits. Your request covered all litigation filed two years before Sam's accident and one year after.

Thirty days passed and you received no response from Acme's counsel. You send a letter on April 1 to counsel reminding him of the request. As there was no response, on May 1, you sent a second demand letter. Finally, on June 15, you filed a motion asking the court to compel discovery. The hearing was set for August 15. On August 1, the insurance company asked the court for a protective order, claiming the request was not relevant and unduly burdensome.

Attached to the petition is an affidavit from an employee of the company stating that to comply with your request, the company must perform a manual search of its records costing upwards of $100,000. Only one verdict in the time period in question has found bad faith on the part of Acme. Acme does have a computerized filing system for most claims.

Your brainstorming board may look like this:

THE LAW	
The request must be relevant to our claim and proportional to the needs of the case.[1] The court may issue an order to protect a party from oppression, undue burden, or expense.	
GOOD FACTS	**BAD FACTS**
March 1 served the request	Will cost $100,000 to produce
There was no answer to first request	Request is for complaints (public records) filed against Acme for bad faith
Wrote a reminder letter on April 1	Documents requested include claim forms that may implicate privacy concerns
There was no response to the letter	The request is for a three-year period
Wrote another letter May 1	Want records after Sam's accident
Opposing counsel did not contact me to resolve this dispute	Only one verdict in the three-year time frame has found that Acme engaged in bad faith
Filed motion on June 15	
Did not hear of the $100,000 cost until the protective order request was filed August 1, two weeks before the hearing	
Most files are computerized	
A manual search is required	A manual search is required

---

1. For this example, we assume that the case is in federal court. Many states' rules will include the magic words "reasonably calculated to result in discoverable materials."

Your factual theory must explain the law, what happened, and why you win. Perhaps your factual theory is:

- The insurance company's pattern of denying valid claims makes it more likely that your client's claim was unjustly denied.

- You did all you could in good faith to resolve this dispute without bothering the court. You waited three and one-half months to ask for the court's help, during which time you wrote to opposing counsel.

- The insurance company did not state its objections to your request until after you filed your motion to compel and advised you of its objection through a court pleading. This precluded you from trying to resolve the problem without the intervention of the court. The insurance company's lack of cooperation is the reason you stand before the court—it should not be rewarded for its conduct.

- It is the insurance company's fault that the cost of retrieving the documents is so expensive. It could easily have stored this information electronically, but chose to keep the files in hard copy only.

1.3   Create Your Theme

A theme is the heart of your case. It explains why you should win and why the judge should care. It is the moral imperative that explains why your claim is just. Your theme is the essence of your argument, stated in one or two sentences. The theme is what you would tell your mother to convince her that you should win your case.

In our example of the motion to compel discovery against the insurance company, a theme may be, "Insurance companies who have a history of bad faith claims continue to deny claims. What is the insurance company hiding here but a pattern of bad faith?" A strong, memorable theme serves as a foundation for an argument, one that grounds you throughout the motion.

Developing a strong theme is discussed in detail in Chapter Three.

1.4   Know Your Timing

Time is important in two respects: how much time do you have to speak, and what time of day is the hearing. Good planning demands you find out the amount of time allocated for your hearing. Preparing for a three-hour motion hearing is very different than planning for a ten-minute one. Most hearings are scheduled for less than thirty minutes. Your goal at those hearings is to make two or three points explaining why you should succeed. Longer hearings allow you more time to expand on the details that support your main points.

From a judge's perspective, it is frustrating to sit through a hearing where the attorney decides to tackle all issues in his papers. Here, the attorney speaks at the judge at supersonic speed. The tendency of the judge is to shut down, not ask any questions, and hope for the presentation to end. To avoid this reaction from the court, make the most of the time you have to speak to the judge. Plan your points carefully. You do not want to merely repeat the points you made in your papers—the judge or her clerk can read them. Pick the points that require further discussion or explanation that you will need to win. Begin your presentation by explaining that because of your limited time, you are resting on the papers for the issues not addressed in this hearing.

Find out what time of day your motion will be heard. Be in the court ready to go fifteen minutes before the hearing is scheduled. Do not get upset if the court is running late. Resist the urge to complain to the judge's staff. Judges do not view time in the same manner as attorneys do and will not appreciate your complaints.

If the motion is to be heard during a "motions call" morning—or as judges affectionately call it, during "cattle call"—you will have the limited attention of the court. Even if the judge has read your papers before the hearing, chances are she may not remember the nuances of your argument or, less charitably, may not remember anything about your motion in the sea of motions she will hear that day. If you are crammed into a motions call, immediately get to the point, be brief, and distinguish yourself in some way. You must stand out from the pack. Make your theme catchy or begin with a clever, yet appropriate, metaphor. But remember, be concise and to the point.

The time of day may also affect the decision of the court. Studies have found that when a judge is hungry or tired, she is more likely to resort to her default position when deciding your motion. In Daniel Kahneman's groundbreaking book, *Thinking Fast and Slow*,[2] he opines that we have two systems of thinking: a fast brain and a slow brain. The fast brain makes decisions with an initial, intuitive "gut call," while the slow brain conducts a careful, thoughtful analysis. He reports a study of the decisions of eight Israeli parole officers. All day these officers heard parole cases. The default decision was to deny parole. The study showed that the officers were more likely to grant a parole request after a morning, lunch, or afternoon break. Nothing explained the increase in releases except that the officers were less hungry and more alert.

This study has implications for an attorney scheduled on a "cattle call" day. If the attorney wants a ruling against the judge's default position, it is best to get the hearing scheduled first thing in the morning or immediately after lunch when the judge is fresh. If that is impossible, the advocate must grab the court's attention with

---

2. Daniel Kahneman, *Thinking, Fast and Slow* (New York: Farrar, Straus and Giroux, 2011).

a memorable theme and then slow down the judge's thinking process. Take time to explain why your case is different than the norm. You can shift the judge from her intuitive gut call and into a deliberate and thoughtful analysis.

1.5   Pick Your Strongest Two or Three Arguments

Your strongest two or three arguments should be independent arguments that support each other. The optimal arguments are like guy wires—strands of inter-twined steel. Each strand is strong, but when knitted together, their tensile strength increases exponentially.

Even if one of your arguments fails, the others will survive. Independent, sup-portive arguments are successful, but domino arguments are not. Be careful of the "domino" arguments, because when one falls, they all fall. To avoid this outcome, always plan for a consistent backup position.

1.5.1   How to Order Your Arguments

Emphasis in oral delivery may be different than the written pleadings. Even though the order of delivery may shift from written to oral delivery, start with your strongest argument. You may not have another chance to showcase it to the judge. Collect your weaker arguments and decide which ones will be chosen for the oral argument. Pick either the weaker arguments that you need to win or the ones the judge will predictably struggle with. Allow the papers to cover the rest, but be pre-pared to address those issues if the court so chooses.

The time spent on your points may be determined by the likelihood of success on that issue. If you know one of your issues is determined law in your jurisdiction, do not waste much time and energy focused on that winning issue. Start with the winner to solidify the agreement between you and the judge, then quickly turn your focus to issues that have a lower likelihood of success.

To keep the court interested, find something of value to argue that was not included in the papers. Maybe it will be a different way of saying the same argu-ment or a different way to frame the issue, but find that twist. You want the judge to leave the hearing thinking the time was well spent.

1.5.2   Prepare to Get to the Point

From a judge's perspective, this may be the most important point of motion advocacy. Get to your point quickly. Judges abhor wasting time, and on busy days they simply do not have the luxury of spending time being led down a seemingly endless path.

Getting to the point takes preparation. Repeatedly cut down your argument until you reach its essence. The essence is the core struggle between the parties and why your client should win. Do not wallow in the detail. Instead, focus on the big picture.

Consider the motion to compel discovery example. Suppose you start out by saying, "We are entitled to receive documents that are relevant and proportional to the needs of the case. Rule 26 says so. The leading case of *Smith v. XYZ* confirms this." The judge is already asleep before you have begun and you have not told her anything that she does not know.

Get to the point to show the court that you honor its time. You will also capture the judge's attention, thereby generating some interest in what you are saying. Instead, try saying, "The insurer hides behind its claim that disclosure is burdensome. Of course it is: the insurance company has painted itself into a corner by not storing its data electronically."

A brief, yet focused argument is no easy task and takes time and preparation. Once you have chosen your arguments, begin by simplifying them for oral delivery. Simple messaging has fewer syllables, memorable phrasing, and eliminates the foundation established in the papers. Your goal is make the judge's job easy—summarize the final take-away point of the argument for her. You will likely be reducing three pages of persuasive writing into three lines of oral delivery.

> **Example**
>
> Practice reducing a written argument into an oral argument. Pick a written motion or response you have authored. Choose the strongest argument for oral delivery. Boil down the argument into a simple, understandable form. Practice delivering this argument in sixty seconds. (*Hint*: A regularly paced delivery should be 165 words per minute.) Can you give the reasons why you win in sixty seconds? In thirty seconds? Take the same argument and change the wording or angle so it does not sound the same.

1.5.3   *Inconsistent Arguments*

Watch out for inconsistent arguments. Judges have the capacity to accept some inconsistency in arguments, but too much inconsistency dilutes the strength of your strongest points. Imagine representing someone charged with murder. At trial you argue: "John did not kill Ann. But if you think he did, it was in self-defense. If you do not believe it was in self-defense, then it was an accident." There comes a time when you dilute the strength of your strongest argument by adding conditions and "if/then" reasoning. It looks like you are hoping that something—anything—sticks.

The logic and the credibility of the advocate are lost with too many inconsistent arguments. There are times when you need inconsistent arguments, but if you have too many contingencies, then the holes in the original proposition become too large.

Exercise

Practice identifying too many inconsistent arguments. Take the following example and note at which step you think the original and strongest argument loses strength.

STEP 1: There was no meeting of the minds for the contract.

STEP 2: If you find there was a meeting of the minds, then there was no consideration.

STEP 3: If you find there was consideration, then the contract is ambiguous.

STEP 4: If you find the contract is not ambiguous, then it is void because of impossibility of performance.

Most listeners would accept Steps 1 and 2, but not Steps 3 or 4. You should not try to "throw too much spaghetti on the wall" in court. Having said this, a Plan B can save you if you sense the judge is disagreeing with you. Pivot to a predetermined fallback position. A fallback position may be a different argument, or it may be a concession that you and your client have agreed upon before the hearing. Usually, presenting a fallback argument is not problematic so long as you do not present a menu of inconsistent arguments that undermine each other.

1.6   Know the Other Side's Case

Once you choose your strongest arguments, step into the shoes of your opponent. Outline his arguments. Anticipate what he will present to the judge. You can never effectively argue your case without knowing the other side. Using the talking points of the opposition allows you to sharpen your chosen arguments and prepare your counterarguments.

For example, as the petitioner in a preliminary injunction motion, you must predict what the respondent will argue to the court. After you have argued that your client is likely to succeed on the merits and that the balance of harms favors him, the respondent might alert the court of the difficulty associated with enforcing such an injunction. As the petitioner, you need to be ready with talking points that preclude the respondent's argument. "Your Honor, enforcing this injunction is no more difficult than enforcing any TRO or injunction. But here, we meet the requirements necessary to grant a preliminary injunction."

1.7 Consider Calling Witnesses

After picking your strongest arguments and understanding the likely arguments of the other side, you may discover that you must call one or more witnesses. With most motions, it is unlikely that calling a witness will be necessary. Many motions are decided on the affidavits, depositions, or other papers submitted to the court before the hearing. However, some motion hearings routinely require testimony, for example, motions to suppress evidence in a criminal setting, or *Daubert* hearings. Examining witnesses is beyond the scope of this book. The same techniques used in court to examine and cross-examine witnesses at trial should be used with witnesses in motion hearings. Make certain you are well versed on these skills.[3]

1.8 Consider Exhibits and Demonstratives

Visual aids and demonstratives are often wrongly forgotten in motion practice. Decide beforehand whether there is an exhibit that will make it easier for the judge to follow your argument. The exhibit must highlight an important point that she must understand for your client to win. The exhibit may be as simple as a copy of the complaint, a map of the area in dispute, a copy of a critical case, a list of documents needed to be produced, excerpts from a deposition, timelines, a decision flowchart, or pictures that focus the court's attention.

Exhibits can be powerful. Simple and clean is always better than complicated. For example, consider a wife's motion to set aside an agreed property settlement because her husband did not disclose the true value of the parties' assets. Wife's counsel may create two foam boards to be displayed side by side to the judge. One foam board itemizes the property disclosed to the wife through discovery, which adds up to a net worth of $1.1 million. The second foam board shows the same property with the values the husband provided to his bank for purposes of obtaining a loan showing the total value at $1.8 million. Only the figures of $1.1 million and $1.8 million are circled on the boards.

The practicality and logistics associated with calling a witness or having demonstratives created and reproduced mean you need to think of them early to avoid a fire drill. Prepare well in advance so you have time to practice with the demonstratives before the motion.

1.9 Anticipate Questions

We have talked about how preparing for a hearing is preparing for spontaneity. The spontaneity generally does not come from the other side, as you have a pretty

---

3. See *Modern Trial Advocacy* for a good discussion on direct and cross-examination techniques. (Steve Lubet & J. C. Lore, *Modern Trial Advocacy*, Fifth Ed. (Boulder: National Institute for Trial Advocacy, 2016.)

good idea from the papers what your opponent will argue. Rather, the spontaneity and its accompanying fear arise from the prospect of the judge asking questions that have not been anticipated.

Questions allow a window into the judge's mind to discover the struggles of the court. When you are asked a question, the court is inviting you to assist in the problem solving. Most judges appreciate attorneys who act as their partners in resolving disputes. Judges ask questions to clear up misunderstandings, clarify thinking, and learn about the facts and the law.

There may be questions that you are unable to answer. With some thoughtful planning, you should be able to anticipate many of the questions that you may be asked. If you can predict the questions, you can prepare the responses to those questions.

Anticipating questions requires you to place yourself in the court's shoes. Think back to the first time that you heard the facts of the case. What questions did you have? What worried you? What struggles did you have? Were the facts the problem? Or was the law the problem? Or, heaven forbid, both? The court is likely to grapple with the same issues. As we delve deeper into a case, our natural tendency is to become more convinced we are right. Take a step back to your initial impressions. From this vantage point, you will be able to anticipate many of the questions the court will have.

Creating a list of potential questions is only the first step; you must also prepare the answers. Chapter Six is devoted to the types of questions you may be asked and how to effectively answer them. If you spend time anticipating likely questions and practicing picture-perfect responses, your comfort level and confidence will increase.

1.10 Be Ready to Negotiate

Judges want to resolve disputes. That is their job. When all opposing attorneys are in one room, there is a chance for resolution. A motion hearing is one of those opportune moments. Judges cannot resist the temptation to negotiate.

The judge may subtly, or not so subtly, direct the parties to negotiate. Who has not heard at the beginning of a hearing, "Counsel, why haven't you settled this case?" Alternatively, in the midst of a hearing, the court may directly negotiate with you: "Counsel, do you really think that the non-compete should be enforced in a fifty-mile radius. Isn't twenty miles sufficient?" In either situation, decide ahead of time if you and your client have a fallback position. Are you willing to accept less than you are asking? This decision must be made beforehand, with your client's approval.

Before the hearing, explain to your client the result of the motion, win or lose. Describe how the judge may push for settlement or a plea deal, or ask for compromises or stipulations. Find out where the client's boundaries lay. Determine how much leeway you have to negotiate on the spot. Explain that this is just a battle in the longer war, and together decide if it is time to die on the sword.

Let us return to the request for all documents pertaining to claims against the insurance company for bad faith. Suppose the court seems to be concerned with the volume and confidentiality of some of the documents you have requested. You may want to consider agreeing with the court that the order should compel only those documents that do not contain confidential information. Or, on the other side of the continuum, you may agree that the order should compel only the names, addresses, and telephone numbers of those people making bad faith claims against the insurer, along with the title of any action filed, the court it was filed in, and the cause number. The final compromise may end somewhere in the middle, and you should obtain your client's consent for any agreement. Your client will be comfortable with a certain range of solutions, and you need to know those boundaries before negotiations start in a hearing.

1.11 Short-Term and Long-Term Consequences

Before you filed your motion, you considered the long-term and short-term consequences of the motion. Is the motion a futile motion both at the trial court level and the appellate level? Is it being filed at the client's insistence? Are you filing it to educate the judge for future motions and it does not matter if you win or lose? Will it only result in a cranky judge for the entirety of the case? Is it dispositive? Is the motion one you are likely to lose at the trial court, but have a reasonable shot at the appellate level? These are all considerations you had to make before you filed the motion.

Your answers to these questions will affect your delivery in the courtroom. Decide before the hearing what tone you will use. If the motion is dispositive, you may be more passionate in your delivery. If you have little likelihood of success at the trial level and are convinced you are destined to appeal, your tone may be the professional tone of one merely making a record.

1.12 Planning Worksheet

Completing this Motion Planning Worksheet before your hearing should help you to clarify your thinking, develop a logical presentation, and anticipate and plan for the unexpected. Ultimately, you need to develop a personalized preparation worksheet that fits your practice and delivery style.

A completed worksheet for our hearing to compel the insurance company to give us documents of previous bad faith claims may look like this:

MOTION PLANNING WORKSHEET	
Legal Elements	***Statute, Cases, Law***
1. Relevant to the claim	Rule 26 (Tab 1)
2. Proportional to need	Rule 37 (Tab 1)
3. Not unduly burdensome	
Critical Good Facts	***Bad Facts***
1. Request for production (Tab 2)	1. Complaints are public
2. March 1 demand (Tab 3)	2. Claims form confidential info
3. April 1 demand (Tab 4)	3. Three years requested (Tab 2)
4. June 15 motion to compel (Tab 5)	4. One verdict against defendant (Tab 7)
5. August 1 protective order first learned of problem (Tab 7)	5. Manual search (Tab 7)
6. $100,000 cost—speculative (Tab 6)	
7. Most files computerized (Tab 7)	

Theme and Sub-Themes		
Insurance company hiding history of bad faith		
Burden is of its own doing		
Time Allotted	***When***	***Where***
10 minutes	August 15 motions call	ND Indiana-Hammond
Witnesses 1. None	***Subpoenaed Date***	***Exhibits*** 1. March 1 demand 2. April 1 demand
Questions		***Responses***
1. How is request proportional to needs?		1. The information is relevant to pattern.
2. How can $100,000 in costs be justified on claim that may be worth less than $100,000?		2. Claim is worth more than $100,000. Even if not, insurance company caused its own problems.

Strongest Argument
Pattern of denying bad faith claims is highly relevant to this bad faith claim.
Argument 2
Burden on the insurance company is of its own doing.
Argument 3
The plaintiff has tried in good faith to resolve this matter outside court; the insurance company has not.
Opponent's Argument 1 and Response
Unduly burdensome. Discovery costs more than the claim.
Insurance company caused burden by keeping claims in hard copy instead of computerizing. Deliberately done in an attempt to hide its bad conduct.

MOTION PLANNING WORKSHEET	
Opponent's Argument 2 and Response	
Request not proportional to the needs of the case.	
Proportional because of the highly relevant nature of the information.	
Opponent's Argument 3 and Response	
Fallback Position	**Client's Approval**
Court pleadings from cases for two years	Yes

See the Appendix for a blank Motion Planning Worksheet. You will find instructions to download the worksheet as a Word document that you can then customize for your own use in motion practice.

1.13 Prepare a Long and a Short Script

Decide how much paper you need to feel comfortable with your oral presentation. Some people are content with thinking through their argument, outlining it in their head, and jotting a few notes on an envelope. Most are not.

An effective tool is to prepare a long script and a short script. A long script is the lengthy version of what you want to say in court, organized by theme, issues, and conclusion. A short script is a condensed version.

Creating a long script clarifies and organizes your thought process. For a typical motion hearing, the spoken long script is seven to ten minutes long, to adapt to the attention span of most people. Ideally, you will never deliver your long script because the judge will be asking you questions about what interests her. But, if the judge is not engaged, you will have the long script as a backup.

Turn your long script into a short script of thirty seconds to three minutes. A rule of thumb is to shorten each page of your long script to one or two sentences. This becomes your "elevator speech"—what you would say to someone during an elevator ride about why you should win your motion. We deal in depth with long and short scripts in Chapter Seven.

1.14 Prepare the Materials You Need for Court

Put together a three-ring binder to take to the lectern when addressing the court. Make sure you can easily open your binder and remove the pages. If your materials are bound like a brief, you will not be able to quickly find the information you need during the hearing.

The opening pages should be the main outline of your argument. Behind those pages, you should have tabs for copies of statutes, rules, or pertinent cases. Likewise, make tabs for depositions, exhibits, affidavits, and other documents you will need to answer the court's factual questions. Alternatively, write your main outline notes in a large-tip marker on the sides of a file folder. For example, if you organize your main outline by issue, devote each side of the folder to an issue. Then create additional file folders for each section that you would tab if you were using a three-ring binder. The goal is to be able to easily retrieve your information.

Find your system of preparing material to bring with you to the podium. Options for preparing materials will be based on the particular motion and your style, and are discussed fully in Chapter Seven.

Note: When we refer to notes throughout this book, we mean paper or electronic. As most courtrooms are becoming digitized, tablets are more widely used by advocates. We still recommend a back-up paper version in case of a technical failure.

CHAPTER TWO

KNOW YOUR AUDIENCE: THE JUDGE

All paths in motion practice lead to a judge. Your presentation must be tailored to the particular judge in your case. To connect with the judge, you must personalize your advocacy. All judges have their strengths, idiosyncrasies, opinions, and attitudes that impact how they see the world and how they will see your case. You may have the most logical, eloquent, and compelling argument, but if it does not speak to your judge, you lose.

Persuasion requires the input of the judge. You provide information and arguments to him, and he processes them through his personal filter and comes to his own conclusions. To convince, you must understand the judge. Persuasion is not telling a judge how he must rule. Rather, persuasion means understanding the judge's view of your case, meeting the judge where he is, and speaking directly to him so he wants to rule in your favor.

All judges are persuaded by credible attorneys who, with conviction, logically argue their positions. We speak at length throughout the book about how to gain and maintain your credibility and logically argue your case with conviction. However, in this chapter, we discuss characteristics peculiar to judges. In particular, we talk about what you should know about the judge and your case—his motivating concerns; his knowledge; his opinions, attitudes, and beliefs; and his relationships with others—and how these factors impact his view of your case. Then we turn to the judge and how he runs his courtroom. Finally, we give you suggestions about how to find and use this knowledge to customize your argument.

2.1 The Judge and His Motivating Concerns

All judges are, to some extent, motivated by fairness, a fear of reversal, a desire for resolution, and the need to be consistent. Speak to one or all of these concerns in your argument or ignore them at your peril. The degree to which you do depends on how much each of these factors influences your judge.

2.1.1 *Fairness and Justice*

Most judges desire to be fair and just in their decisions. Judges want to get it right. They want to leave the courthouse at the end of the day with a sense of satisfaction.

They want to be respected for ruling justly. Well-intentioned attorneys and judges often disagree on what should be considered fair in a case. Respectfully convincing the judge of your position and assuming he desires fairness will achieve the best long-term results for you and your client. Do not underestimate how the draw of a just and fair result impacts a ruling. Because fairness is subjective, your job is to convince the judge that a result in your client's favor is the right decision—a decision he can be proud of.

All judges were trained—as all attorneys are—to think logically and follow the law. Certainly your argument should appeal to the judge's analytical mind. Logic and law are an important part of a decision, but in many cases, the law is flexible enough to allow the judge to rule for either party. This is particularly so at a trial court level, where the judge is the sole determiner of the facts and has broad discretion. Law is more than logic; it is about people, right and wrong, good and bad. Link your vision of fairness with the law and the facts so the judge sees it your way.

After making your logical case, follow the logic with an appeal to justice. The blatancy of the appeal depends on the judge and the facts of the case. Some judges are more amenable to these pleas than others. Because appeals to fairness are appeals to the emotions of a judge, tread lightly. No matter the judge, begin by using subtle appeals to fairness. Naked appeals to emotions, before laying a logical foundation, generally backfire, as a judge views sound decisions as reasoned ones, not emotional ones.

Earn the right to preach an emotional point and wait for the right facts to present themselves. One way to earn the right to speak emotionally is to avoid using hyperbole. You are more likely to be believed that "all interrogatories are lacking" if you have previously avoided using "always, never, all, and completely" for emphasis. Over-exaggeration is a dangerous way to cry wolf. It makes it hard to deliver a believable emotional argument when you have over-inflated most points along the way.

Indirectly appeal to a judge's sense of fairness through your theme. A theme tells the court why your client should win and why it should matter to the court. Usually, the theme speaks to a judge's inner sense of fairness and justice. For example, "Equity does not reward those with unclean hands" and the petitioner has "unclean hands because . . ." makes clear that a ruling for the petitioner would be unfair. Yet, at the same time, it addresses the very issue the judge must resolve. Likewise, in a discovery dispute using a theme such as "They are asking for too much, with too little value, at too high a cost," tells the court where justice lay.

Dealing with the facts also gives you an opportunity to delicately appeal to the justice of the case. Tell the facts of your motion in a story from your client's vantage point. Where legitimate, portray your client as the good guy who was wronged because of the actions of the other side. Persuade the judge that a ruling in your favor will resolve the conflict in a just and fair manner.

Near the end of your argument, after you have argued why the law demands a ruling in your favor, argue the fairness for your client. By then, you have shown that reason and logic demand your result and so too does fairness and justice. This plea comes at the end of your presentation before the prayer for relief. The plea, the call to duty, is designed to make the judge proud of his decision and gives him the strength to do the right thing. The call to duty must be delivered with conviction. If you do not believe in your case, neither will the judge. Show you have confidence in your position; your enthusiasm will be contagious.

2.1.2 *Reversal*

Judges generally do not want to be reversed. Some judges disdain reversal, while others are merely annoyed by it. The level of sensitivity depends on a judge's personality or his ambitions. Nevertheless, all judges are sensitive, even if slightly so, to being reversed. You must appeal to that concern. The judge who may be indifferent to reversal may not be persuaded, but it is worth a try, as you are also appealing to the interest of the judge to follow the law. In any event, all appeals to a judge's concern for reversal should be indirect.

No matter what, do not say to the court, "I am going to take you up on appeal if you rule against me."[1] Statements like that only make the judge more resolute in his conviction. Do you imagine after threatening appeal a judge will say, "Oh, I now see the light. You're right. I'll reverse my position"? The odds are highly unlikely. With a challenge like this, the judge usually says, "Go ahead." When you alert him of your intention to appeal, he is usually more careful with his written findings. Remember, a judge is the sole decider of credibility, and your threat may have inspired the judge to find facts unfavorable to your position, making a successful appeal difficult. Threats to appeal are not only unsuccessful, but they also reduce your chances of a reversal on appeal.

How, then, do you appeal to a judge's sensitivity to reversal? If the law is on your side, wrap yourself around precedent. Glue yourself to it. Identify quotes of well-respected jurists who support your position. Identify the author of the quote, who may be the judge you are before. Explain that the case before him is squarely on all fours with another case that supports your argument.

Argue the standard of review ever so lightly. Attorneys seldom think in terms of the standard of review on appeal because so few cases are appealed, but judges know the drill. If the appellate court engages in de novo review, a judge is much more likely to be reversed than if the higher court reviews for an abuse of discretion. Argue that what you are asking is within the broad discretion of the judge. Empower the judge,

---

1. Every experienced trial attorney has one story of how threatening an appeal worked on a judge. The operative word here is "one." With years of experience and the credibility to back it up, the threat may succeed for the veteran, who delivers the message with style and elegance.

appeal to his pride and discretion. However, if you are pushing the limits of the law, argue that the relief you request is in line with the natural progression of the law or gives the judge a golden opportunity to be a pioneer.

On the other hand, if opposing counsel is asking for relief that may be legally weak, tell the court the relief the other side asks for is without precedent. Explain that no reported case has provided such broad relief. You can discourage the judge from being a pioneer by casting the move in a risky light. Try the alternatives below.

SENSITIVITY TO REVERSAL	
"Our case is on all fours with *Smith*."	"A long line of cases hold that . . ."
"There is nothing new here, the case of . . ."	"Judge Learned Hand said of this . . ."
"The leading case in this area . . ."	"This is within your discretion, Your Honor."
"The relief the other side asks for is unprecedented."	"No reported case has ever provided such broad relief."

2.1.3   *Concern for Time and an Overloaded Docket*

All judges in all cases want resolution. You may think that is an overstatement. It is not. Judges are busy; their job is to resolve conflicts in an efficient way. Judges understand this mission. What is more, every year, a judge creates a statistical report distributed to the public that shows the number of cases he closed and the number of cases still pending. All judges are evaluated, in part, by their peers, themselves, and their superiors on these numbers.

This is not to say that a judge favors resolution over justice. In other words, a valid claim will not be dismissed by the judge for the sake of his numbers. But if the claim is meritless, then dispositive motions, such as dismissals or summary judgments, are an attractive avenue for a judge to take. If you are asking the court to grant a dispositive motion, then note for the court that the ruling will end the case.

Even if the motion is not dispositive, show the judge how to use the motion to encourage the parties to settle. Indicate to the court how a ruling in your favor will facilitate settlement. Or show the court that ruling for your opponent will likely result in future headaches for the judge. If you doubt you will prevail on the motion, encourage the court to take a ruling under advisement pending negotiations.

To the judge overly concerned with his congested docket, hit hard on how a ruling for your client may facilitate an ending to the case. Even for the judge unconcerned with time efficiencies, appeal to his interest to resolve the case by showing him the path forward.

APPEALING TO RESOLUTION
"Granting our motion will bring this case closer to resolution—one way or another."
"This motion is dispositive because . . ."
"A ruling in our favor will substantially narrow the issues."
"A ruling for [insert issue] will bring all parties to the settlement table."
"A ruling for the other side will create an enforcement nightmare."

2.1.4 Desire for Consistency in Rulings

Judges want to be predictable—some more than others. Predictability is important to attorneys and their ability to advise clients. Attorneys advise businesses and individuals to chart a course of conduct or avoid another based upon the probability of an outcome. Judges know this. Predictability also makes a judge's life easier because parties settle their cases based upon their expectations of a judge's ruling.

Most judges also want to be internally consistent. Where appropriate, appeal to a judge's desire to issue rulings that are consistent with what he has ruled in the past. Argue that ruling for you will be consistent with the way he ruled in a similar case and therefore gives predictability to the attorneys who appear before him. Also, you may argue that the case is a typical case that should result in a typical ruling—one he has decided in the same manner many times before. Alternatively, if you do not want the court to follow a normal course, argue how atypical this case is based on the facts.

A JUDGE'S MOTIVATING CONCERNS AND YOUR CASE	
Reasoned decisions	*Tell why the facts and law compel a win.*
Fairness and justice	*Use themes. Facts in story. Direct appeal to fairness only after the logical argument.*
Fear of reversal	*Glue yourself to precedent. Argue the court's discretion.*
Desire to resolve	*Show the path forward, smooth or bumpy, after the ruling.*
Desire for consistency in rulings	*Refer to prior decisions of the judge consistent with the ruling you want. Or distinguish the case from the norm.*

2.2 A Judge and His Knowledge: A Sliding Scale

What the judge knows when he walks into the courtroom for your hearing will significantly affect your presentation. Talking to a prepared judge is different than talking to one who is ill-prepared. Likewise, discussions with an expert in the law are on a different plane than discussions with a novice.

2.2.1 *Reads Nothing, Little, or Everything*

What has your judge read before the hearing? Has he pored over every paper you filed and researched the cases cited? Has he cursorily reviewed your papers? Or has he read nothing? Although you never will really know beforehand, most judges follow a pattern. Find out the judge's habits.

Make an educated guess about the amount of preparation the judge has done. Do not ask the judge if he has read the papers. That question reveals what you think of the judge—he is unprepared. The judge will not appreciate it.

Prepare to dig deeper into the cases and facts with a prepared judge. He does not want you to merely repeat the content of the pleadings. He wants to probe the nuances of the arguments. Even so, do not forego the crucial facts of your case with the well-informed judge. Tell the facts in a story to him. Know the two or three key cases cold. Be able to discuss the similarities and dissimilarities with the facts in your case.

The typically ill-prepared judge will probably not disappoint expectations in your case. Prepare a thirty-second fact wrap-up, and dive in without fanfare:

"Here's how we got here, Your Honor . . ."

"To sum up the course of events so far . . ."

"As Your Honor knows . . ."

"To recap . . ."

Rely heavily on the magic words found in the cases. To learn auditory information for the first time is difficult for anyone, let alone to absorb the subtleties of a complicated argument in a limited time. Keep your arguments simple and clear.

No judge wants to look stupid. Regardless of whether the judge is prepared, do not talk down to him. Do not mock or belittle a question from the bench. Do not say, "That is not the issue here, the better question is . . .," or "This is an interesting question, but not relevant here." After a dumb question, do not give the judge a shocked look. Keep your poker face and answer the question as best you can.

Make the judge appear smart by using his words in your argument. When answering a question, weave the judge's words into your answer. Take this exchange, for example:

Judge: Counsel, isn't personal jurisdiction met here?

Counsel: Yes, Your Honor, personal jurisdiction is met here.

Use the judge's words in other parts of your argument as well:

Counsel: As the judge said when discussing this with my colleague, "the issue boils down to the amount of the contacts in the jurisdiction. The contacts here show . . ."

The techniques to answer questions will be explored further in Chapter Six.

2.2.2   *Expertise in Area of Law*

Your judge may know nothing about the law in your case, may know a moderate amount, or may be an expert in the field. Find out where on the spectrum of knowledge your judge lies.

If the judge is a novice in the area of law, spend some time explaining the law. Tell him the reasons the law is so written. Talk to him about the law; do not lecture. Put your explanation in plain words. Simplify without talking down to him. Do not preface your sentences with, "Let me explain to you . . . ." Do not slow your cadence down to a crawl thinking that the judge needs slowness to capture your point. Do not robotically repeat the same point using the same words. Instead, mimic the most engaging teacher you have seen.

On common issues that are likely to often come before the court, do not waste your time on the basics. Instead, zero in on the flashpoint. For example, on a motion for a preliminary injunction, do not waste time outlining the elements that must be proven by the petitioner. If your strongest argument is that the petitioner is unlikely to succeed on the merits, go directly there.

If a judge is an expert in the area of law, there is no need to begin with the basics. Plunge head first into the conflict. Plan to have a profound discussion on the issue. Plan for more than a superficial conversation about the law and focus on your facts.

Expert in the area of law or not, many judges need help with the practicalities of the case. It may have been a long time since the judge practiced in the area or he may have never practiced in the field. Tell him how it actually works in the real world and the consequences of his ruling. He relies on you for that expertise. Give him your know-how. When done properly, this becomes a way to collaborate with the judge so he joins your cause.

2.3   A Judge and Opinions, Attitudes, and Beliefs

Life experiences result in opinions, attitudes, and beliefs. Two people can see the same homeless person walking down a city street in an entirely different way. One is convinced the person is lazy and an alcoholic, undeserving of a handout. The other is convinced the person is down on his luck, mentally ill, and in need of help. All of us, including judges, view the world through the prism of our experiences.

2.3.1   *Judicial Philosophy*

Judges form strong opinions about legal issues. Those opinions may have been formed in law school, or may have been formed through practicing law. But judges, like most people, have attitudes and beliefs that shape their judgments. Judges may have been public defenders or prosecutors, sometimes both. They may have practiced either plaintiff's personal injury work or insurance defense. Whatever their prior experience, they developed judicial philosophies.

Judges also have views on procedural matters. Some judges are liberal in discovery; others are not. Some judges are more likely to grant summary judgment, dismissals, or default judgments. Some are generous on attorney fee awards, while others are stingy.

Learn your judge's preferences on the issues of your case. If the judge is prone to agreeing with your position, use it to your advantage without flaunting it. If you are not so lucky, find a common ground and build from there. Begin by starting with the judge's preference on the issue, and then differentiate your case. For example, if the judge generally grants discovery requests, begin by explaining that most discovery should be granted. With this start, you align yourself with the judge, making it more likely that he will listen to your argument. But, then explain why this is not the typical discovery case.

Consider this sample language:

> *Counsel*: Your Honor, I understand that discovery should be liberal in most instances. Open discovery normally promotes settlement. While discovery should generally be liberal, here disclosure would interfere with confidential attorney–client privilege and work product. In this shareholder-derivative action, the shareholders are demanding the complete written report of the special-litigation committee. The report was prepared to determine whether to pursue the shareholder's claims. We have provided the report to the shareholders, but redacted those portions of the report prepared by the corporation's counsel advising the committee of the likelihood of the suit's success. The material deleted from the report is attorney–client privileged information and work product in preparation of litigation. We've given them what we could.

2.3.2 Conservative versus Liberal Views

Political views impact judges' decisions. Reams have been written by political scientists about the effect of conservative and liberal beliefs on the decisions of appellate courts and the United States Supreme Court. Less has been printed on the influence on trial court judges.[2] Nevertheless, trial court judges have considerable discretion in determining the facts and applying the law, allowing political views to influence their decision making.

---

2. For a scholarly work summarizing this issue read, *What's Law Got to Do with It? What Judges Do, Why They Do It, and What's at Stake*, by Charles Gardner Geyh (Stanford: Stanford University Press, Stanford, 2011).

Where a judge lies on the continuum of political views impacts all judgments. In criminal sentencing, admissibility of evidence, and dismissals, the conservative judge is more likely to impose stricter sentences, less likely to suppress the government's evidence, and less likely to dismiss an indictment. Political views impact business cases with liberal judges more likely to hold against a corporation and tending to be more favorable to plaintiffs in personal injury cases and medical malpractice cases.[3]

Judges cross party lines issue by issue. Some may be conservative in criminal cases, yet liberal on cases involving corporations and personal injuries. Determine where your judge stands on the political spectrum regarding your issue. Begin by aligning yourself with the judge's view, then either convince the judge that a favorable ruling aligns with his philosophy or gradually pull the judge toward your position. Argue the other factors that influence the judge—such as concern for resolution, reversal, and fairness—hoping that those factors will override the conservative, moderate, or liberal viewpoint.

2.4 A Judge and His Relationships with Others

Knowing a judge's relationships with others and his preconceptions about various types of attorneys is helpful information to know before arguing your motion.

2.4.1 Elected or Appointed

When standing for election, a judge may be swayed by public opinion on issues before him that are of public concern. Depending on the judge, the time in the cycle of his election, or the issue, the election may or may not have an impact on his decision. An appointed judge can also be influenced in his decision making by the importance of the decision to the party or parties responsible for his appointment.

Be aware of these potential influences. Argue the other interests of the judge aggressively to counterbalance the effect of politics. Justice, fairness, and the rightness of the ruling tug strongly on a judge concerned with political affairs because his future could be at stake.

2.4.2 Alignment of the Judge with Opposing Counsel or You

Sometimes the judge will have a relationship with the attorney on the other side of the case. Relationships vary—maybe they belong to the same Inn of Court, maybe they practiced law together at one time, maybe they serve on the same board of a charitable organization. Relationships can be worrisome for a number of reasons. First, the attorney knows what is likely to persuade the judge and how

---

3. Many works do not define liberalism and conservatism in the context of trial judges. Even though USLAW does not define these concepts, its website at uslaw.org classifies every county in each state by liberal, moderate, or conservative benches.

to push those buttons. Second, the court likely finds the attorney credible and so the attorney's arguments carry extra weight with the judge. Third, the relationship may engender favoritism—but remember, it may also create animosity. Short of recusal, there is not much you can do but be aware of the relationship. If you show the judge that you are not ruffled by the relationship and assume he will be fair despite the connection, you will earn the judge's respect.

If you are the attorney with a relationship with the judge, avoid presumptive behavior instigating a familiar tone. You do not want opposing counsel to pine away for recusal, nor do you want to act aloof with a judge who knows you outside the courtroom. To strike the right balance, behave respectfully and confidently and respond in a friendly manner when and if the judge refers to your history together.

Likewise, judges have preconceptions about various types of attorneys. Some judges favor attorneys from large law firms, while others favor attorneys from small firms. Maybe your judge is inclined toward more experienced attorneys over less experienced ones or local counsel over out-of-town counsel. If you are not in a position to add the type of attorney favored by your judge to your team, then buck the stereotype about the type of attorney disfavored by the judge. As the out-of-town attorney, faithfully follow all local rules with alacrity, including any dress code preferences.

THE JUDGE AND THE CASE	
Reads everything or reads nothing	*Prepare to dig deep into the issue with the prepared judge. Have a thirty-second fact wrap-up for the ill prepared. Do not make the judge look stupid.*
Expert in the area or novice	*If an expert, no need for the basics. Delve in the issue. If a novice, spend time explaining the law and its reasons. No lecturing.*
Judicial philosophy in area	*Identify it. Start with the judge's opinion, and then differentiate the case from the norm.*
Conservative or liberal	*Identify it. Convince the judge that ruling aligns with his view. Argue other factors that may influence the ruling.*
Elected versus appointed	*Recognize the influence. Argue justice, fairness, and the correctness of the ruling in your favor.*
Alignment with opposing counsel or you	*Consider change of judge or recusal depending on the relationship. Buck the stereotype the judge has about the type of attorney you are.*

2.5   The Judge and the Courtroom

Learn the judge's courtroom procedures. Adapt your presentation to the judge's preferences.

2.5.1   Informal versus Formal

Some judges handle motion hearings very casually. Some even hold the hearings in chambers. If the hearing is held in chambers, the good news is that you will be more relaxed and able to better connect to the judge and his concerns. The bad news is that often these in-chamber discussions are not recorded. For any number of reasons, including the possibility that your client may want to appeal, you need to preserve an accurate record.

If you find yourself in an informal chamber and need to capture the discussion, politely ask for the court reporter to join you or ask that the hearing be held on the record in the courtroom. If you absolutely know you will win and have no intention of appealing, then go with the flow and let the other side take the heat for being record-hungry.

In the courtroom, some judges are very informal while others are formal. You will rarely offend a judge by erring on the side of respectful decorum in delivery and dress. Even if the judge prefers a more casual atmosphere, treat every party with good manners and present yourself in a polished, professional way.[4] A courtroom is a judge's office. Consider yourself a guest in his space and act accordingly.

If the judge conducts formal hearings, follow the protocol. Some judges are task-masters for decorum in a courtroom. Unwritten and written rules abound about how attorneys are to conduct themselves: be timely; rise when speaking to a judge; deliver your argument behind the podium; address the judge as "Your Honor" or "Judge [insert surname]"; do not disparage opposing counsel; and direct all arguments to the judge, not opposing counsel. If your judge is a stickler for obedience in the courtroom, disobedience can be costly. The judge may believe that you are being disrespectful to him and to the institution. Your credibility will be diminished.

Do not confuse formality with coldness. A more formal judge may be more concerned with efficiency and knows that formality keeps things moving on a motions day. Judges appreciate your adherence to the rules as a sign of respect. Certain judges tolerate a little deviation from the rules, which allows you more flexibility in your argument. For example, some judges permit you to speak even when not called upon. Others allow you to speak beyond your time. In the more laidback court, if the judge is particularly interested in a topic, sur-rebuttal and sur-sur-rebuttal arguments are routine. Often the judge will invite sur-rebuttal, even with only a slight glance in your direction; sometimes not. But if the judge is interested, the conversation may continue well beyond your preordained turn.

The judge who prefers a more casual atmosphere will encourage more small talk, include his clerks in conversation during a proceeding, and readily switch the

---

4. Be careful to dress proportionately to your client or the opposing party. If your client is being sued by a nonprofit, best to avoid wearing the Armani suit and cufflinks to court.

schedule at a hearing depending on the circumstances. This requires an advocate to be flexible. Even if the judge is more casual in the courtroom, show him respect. For example, the practice may be that the attorneys sit at counsel table while presenting their arguments. Even so, do not address the judge while sitting. Out of respect for the judge and the position, rise to your feet. Standing indicates how serious you are taking the matter. If he asks you to remain seated, then comply.

2.5.2 Humor

Most judges want to have some fun. An attorney should not think of himself as a stand-up comedian, but it is important to be energetic and entertaining. The next time a judge falls asleep during your motion, consider that the problem may be you. Craft interesting phrases. Be creative in problem-solving. Make exhibits colorful. Have energy in your voice, stressing what is important so the judge will follow your lead. Distinguish yourself from the mass of attorneys he has seen that day. You want the judge to say to himself, "That was well done. This is why I do this for a living."

Always laugh at a judge's joke. Laugh with the same intensity the judge does—not more or less. Do not out-humor a judge. A little self-deprecation can be effective, but avoid false humility. For example, do not pretend to be less intelligent than you are: "Your Honor, I can hardly understand this regulation." Instead: "I can understand the regulation, but the engineer on the ground can't consult with me every time a government change order is needed to complete the electrical project."

There are certain types of humor that should always be avoided. Do not use humor at the expense of the parties or other counsel. Avoid sarcasm in general, and never engage in racial, gender-based, or cultural jokes.

Beyond that, it depends on the judge. If you are before a judge who appreciates the clever exchange between quick-thinking trial attorneys, employ a reasonable amount of taciturn exchanges and humor. But, the humor should not be prearranged; it should come naturally from the circumstances of the hearing. If used properly, humor energizes a bored judge, makes your arguments memorable, and reveals you to be the intelligent and clever person you are.

2.5.3 The Overworked Motions-Call Judge

Motions-call day means the judge's brain is on overload. The courtroom is full of litigants and their attorneys, patiently (or impatiently) waiting their turn. Numerous hearings are held—one after another, without a break. During the hearing, the judge is listening to your argument while at the same time signing agreements that have been reached by other litigants scheduled that day. In a word: chaos. Get to the point quickly.

2.5.4   Law Clerk

Many judges have a law clerk who listens to the arguments and helps write the judge's order. Some judges heavily rely on their clerk; others not.

If a writing clerk is present during the hearing and the judge relies on the clerk for research and/or her opinion, you may be speaking to two audiences. During your argument, your eye contact should remain with the judge. You do not want the judge to think that you believe his clerk is more important than he is. But, you may briefly look at the clerk to see her reaction when you release your eye contact from the judge or when the judge is reading. This technique is important if the judge runs a more casual courtroom and likes to include the clerk. If that is the case, then occasionally make eye contact with the clerk.

When your opponent argues, you will be able to survey both the judge's and clerk's reactions to your opponent's arguments. You may also catch some of the non-verbal communication between them. The nonverbal information you gain may allow you to modify the direction of your argument and craft your rebuttal.

2.5.5   The Extent of the Judge's Questioning

Your judge may or may not be an active questioner. If the judge is known to be an active questioner, odds are that you will be extensively questioned. Prepare for that reality. On the other hand, if you know the judge to be a silent observer, prepare to monologue.

THE JUDGE AND THE COURTROOM	
Formal versus informal	*Stick to formality even if in an informal setting. Make sure you get your record.*
Decorum in the court	*Stick to the rules with the judge who demands obedience. Energize the courtroom with your enthusiasm. Laugh at the judge's jokes. Sparingly use self-deprecation.*
Motions-call versus time certain	*The shorter the time and the more chaos, the simpler and more succinct.*
Law clerk	*Depending on if the judge relies on a clerk, you may be speaking to a second audience.*
Active questioner versus no questions	*If active, spend time predicting questions and answers. If no questions, have a bullet point prepared script and watch the judge.*

2.6   The Judge's Personality

The more that you know about a judge, the better you can modify your arguments to speak directly to him. Here are suggestions on how to deal with some common personality traits of a judge.

THE JUDGE'S PERSONALITY	
Cautious	*Give the judge courage to rule in your favor. The law is settled, the ruling is fair and right.*
Easy-to-change positions	*Keep the conversation going. Try for the last word. Ask for sur-rebuttal.*
Thinks out loud	*Listen. Adapt your argument to what you hear.*
Processes silently	*Do not be concerned. Watch the judge for nonverbal cues.*[5]
Big picture	*Paint the landscape. Do not drill down to the details.*
Detail oriented	*Make sure you correctly state the facts and law. No errors.*
Industrious	*Help the judge write the order. At the end, tell him what you want and how to get there.*
Creative	*Propose creative solutions.*
Lazy	*Prepare impressive findings of fact and conclusions of law. Track your argument to the proposed order.*
Curt	*Do not let it shake you. He is curt to everyone.*
Ambitious	*Show him that he will not be reversed on appeal by ruling for you—and a ruling for you is within the mainstream.*
Shoots from the hip	*Try to slow down the argument. Slow your pace. Appeal to broad principles of fairness and justice.*

2.7 How Do You Research the Judge?

If you have been in front of the judge numerous times before, you will not have to do much research. Better yet, if you have served as a law clerk for him or for a colleague of his, then you have even more insight. However, if you do not know the judge, use the resources at your disposal to gather information.

Go online. Read the judge's decisions. Look at the court's website and his biography to learn what the judge wants you to know. Search for his name online. You will be surprised what you may learn from a simple internet search. This may provide newspaper articles about him, speeches he has made, or his favorite community organizations. You may find out he has ambitions for a higher court or that he is in limbo, awaiting appointment, at the time of your hearing. Go to

---

5. These techniques are covered in Chapters Six, Seven, and Nine.

www.therobingroom.com, a website where attorneys rate and comment on judges. Use the various litigation services available on the internet that profile judges.

Talk to attorneys in your firm or your attorney friends. Send an email advising them that you will be appearing before the judge and asking them if they have any insight into the judge. Write the email in a way that if it is forwarded to the judge you will not be embarrassed. Likewise, ask for a phone call in return, as opposed to an email response.

Talk to former clerks. Make blind calls to attorneys whose names appear on the court's decisions. Research the local bar's ratings of him.

Go to the courtroom. Sit through a proceeding. File a pleading directly with the court staff. Engage in small talk with the court staff about the judge's favored practices.

Go to the judicial qualifications board in your state and get a copy of his statement of economic interest. Each year, a judge must file a report indicating income and gifts he receives from any source. If the judge is elected, go to the local election board and get a copy of his campaign financing report. It will tell you who has contributed to the judge's election campaign.

If your client has the resources available, hire local counsel, someone who has repeatedly been in the court.

2.8   Putting It All Together

To see how to pull all of the elements we've discussed in this chapter into a rhetorical strategy for addressing a judge, consider the Elephant, Inc. scenario below. Then study the tables and graphics that follow the narrative to track how we built an effective strategy for facing the judge in this case.

You represent the Green family in their dispute against Elephant, Inc. Elephant, Inc. travels the country staging their renowned Elephant Extravaganza. The Extravaganza is held in a three-ring circus tent, where twenty elephants perform feats never before seen by circus audiences. Unfortunately, the elephants make quite a mess inside and outside the tent. Each morning, afternoon, and evening of a performance, a three-man crew cleans the tent and its surroundings by spraying Elephant-a-Clean on the tent floor, elephant cages, circus rings, and apparatus. Elephant-a-Clean contains toxins known to cause bronchiolitis obliterans and other respiratory illnesses in workers spraying it.

Mayor Green, his wife, and two children—Matthew, age ten, and Charlotte, age eight—attended the May 20 performance of Elephant Extravaganza in their home town of Pachydermia, Oregon. The Greens arrived early to the performance and sat ten feet from the center ring in the front row, where approximately five minutes earlier the workers sprayed Elephant-a-Clean. Two days later, both children experienced a dry cough, shortness of breath, and wheezing. One year later, after the children's symptoms worsened, a lung biopsy established that they developed bronchiolitis obliterans (BO), a disease characterized by progressive decline in pulmonary function.

The Green family hired you to represent them in a personal injury suit. To prove general causation, Dr. Ayre, a prominent toxicologist specializing in airborne toxins, will testify that Elephant-a-Clean is capable of causing the children's injuries. Dr. Ayre bases his opinion on a study that the toxins in Elephant-a-Clean can cause BO in workers repeatedly exposed to it. Extrapolating from those studies, Dr. Ayre opines that because of the children's tender age, even the limited exposure they had to Elephant-a-Clean could cause BO. To prove specific causation, Dr. Smith, the children's pediatrician, will testify that before the circus, the children had no respiratory problems.

Elephant, Inc. moves in limine to exclude Dr. Ayre's opinion, challenging the reliability of his "scientific" method under *Daubert*. Dr. Ayre's opinion is your sole evidence on general causation, and if excluded, the court must grant summary judgment for Elephant, Inc. There is no case in your jurisdiction that allows an expert to extrapolate general causation from a group repeatedly exposed to a toxin to a group with limited exposure. The standard of review is an abuse of discretion.

The judge who will decide this case is an expert in evidence law. He is very sensitive to being reversed, even more so because he stands for re-election later this year. He is known to be liberal and is a member of the same political party as Mayor Green. Before taking the bench, he was a plaintiff's personal injury attorney for fifteen years. He efficiently disposes of his cases but not at the expense of fairness, justice, and victims' rights.

You consult a colleague who has argued before him, who tells you that the judge has a keen legal mind and actively questions the attorneys. You are set for an all-day evidentiary hearing. He runs his courtroom in a formal manner and has no law clerk. The judge reads everything, is somewhat of a stickler for the rules, and is moderately deadpan.

A spectrum graph of the judge, his concerns, interests, and proclivities would look like the following.

The Judge

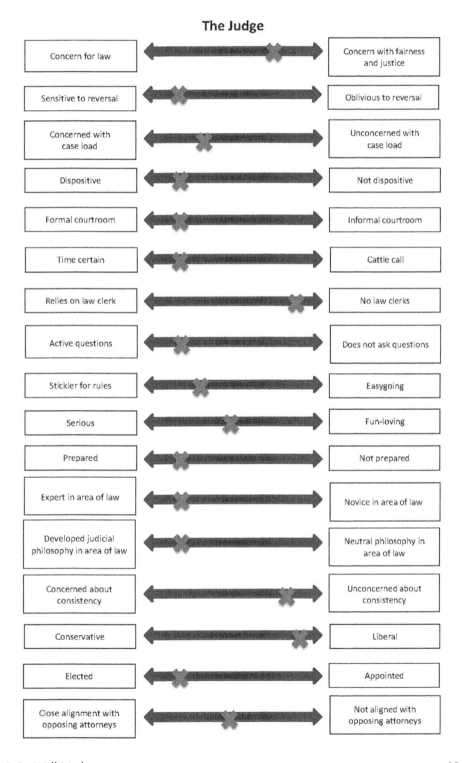

Tailoring Your Presentation

PLAINTIFF	
Sensitivity to reversal	*Emphasize the clear abuse of discretion standard of review. Evidentiary rulings are generally within the purview of the trial court judge.*
Expert in area of law	*Discuss the history of Daubert. (Daubert is intended to liberalize the admission of expert testimony.)*
Concern for fairness	*Make sure that the story is from Matthew's and Charlotte's perspective. Stress the proximity in time from the circus to three days later, when the respiratory problems began. Emphasize the expertise of Dr. Ayre.*
Concern for consistency	*Predictability of law is less important than the right and fair outcome.*
Judicial philosophy on personal injury suits	*Highlight the right for the injured to have a jury trial. Do this after the legal case. The judge understands the stakes with a mention—no need to pull too hard at his heart strings.*
Dispositive motion	*Underscore that this is a dispositive motion. Without causation evidence, the court must grant the defendant's summary judgment.*
Concern for resolution	*Fairness and justice are more important to this judge. Because this is dispositive, concern for efficiencies are probably irrelevant.*
Active questioner who has read everything	*Bring legal discussion to platitudes—philosophy behind Daubert is for increased admissibility of expert opinion. Show although no case law authorizes extrapolation, given the expertise of Dr. Ayre and the short time between exposure and symptoms, the natural progression of the law would admit the testimony.*
Formal courtroom/serious demeanor	*Follow all protocol. Formal is good, as we need a record. Display the seriousness of this motion with your tone.*
Elected	*The judge will expect this to make the newspaper because of the mayor's involvement. Because this is an election year and the judge is the same political party as the mayor, it may have an impact. Behind the scenes, manage the public relations tactfully. To the judge, make no mention of the connection.*

National Institute for Trial Advocacy

Tailoring Your Presentation

DEFENDANT	
Sensitivity to reversal	*Stress that no case has ever allowed extrapolation of one study to a dissimilar factual situation. This is not reliable science. What the plaintiff asks is unprecedented in this or any jurisdiction. Cite cases where trial courts have been reversed on Daubert rulings to show abuse of discretion is not a license to err.*
Expert in area of law	*Go back to Federal Rule of Evidence 702 and its demand that the testimony must be the product of reliable scientific principles and methods. Just because Dr. Ayre says it is so is not enough. Highlight the facts of Dr. Ayre's method—not the facts of the injury. Cite cases where the court has explained reliable scientific methodology. Argue the facts of those cases. Show that none use extrapolation. Get into the weeds of the law.*
Concern for fairness	*Acknowledge that the sympathies lie with the kids, but the ruling must be based on the law. Keep bringing the court back to the law.*
Concern for consistency	*Predictability of law is important for this case and others who may become before him.*
Judicial philosophy on personal injury suits	*Understand the tragedy of the kids, but it is not our fault. Give him the courage to do his duty. If causation could be found with expert testimony, surely able plaintiff's counsel would find the expert. No one exists.*
Dispositive motion	*Yes, but must follow the law. We are not at summary judgment stage yet. This motion is narrow, we must stick to the issues presently before the court.*
Concern for resolution	*Have a settlement number ready to offer the judge and opposing counsel. Emphasize that the plaintiff is unlikely to prevail at a jury trial and as a matter of law.*
Active questioner who has read everything	*Choose two to three cases that highlight what is needed for a reliable scientific method. Know the facts cold. Contrast those facts with the lack of method Dr. Ayre used.*
Formal courtroom/sober demeanor	*Follow protocol. No humor whatsoever. This is serious business.*
Elected	*Include a call to duty after the logical argument recognizing that it is a tough case because children are involved. It particularly strikes close to home because the mayor's children are involved, but exclusion is the right decision.*

Exercise

Plan your next motion hearing. Fill out the spectrum graph. Decide how to tailor your argument to the judge.

The Judge

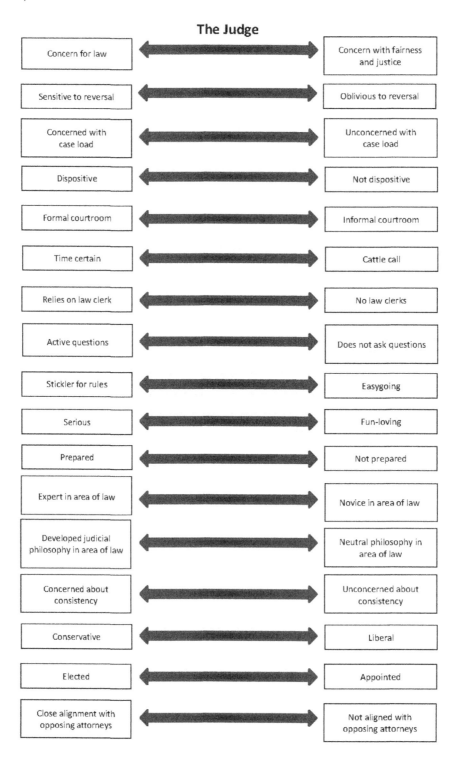

CHAPTER THREE

THEMES: THE *WHAT*, THE *WHY*, AND THE *HOW*

Themes have long been used effectively in trial work. The most well-known theme in modern legal history is largely remembered by all attorneys, young and old, more than twenty years later: "If it doesn't fit, you must acquit." This theme worked and became the mantra of the O. J. Simpson case worldwide because it simplified a complex issue, evoked a picture, and was memorable.

Likewise, themes are essential in oral arguments before a judge. This chapter explores what themes are, why they are important, what constitutes a good theme, how to create them, and what to do with them.

3.1 The *What*

A theme is the main point—the take-away of the motion of the case. If you had to boil down your case to one, two, or three sentences, what would you say? A theme is the essence of your argument—why you should win. It is a powerful pithy statement that explains not only the logic of your argument, but also the heart of your argument—why the judge should care about ruling for you. The theme summarizes the entire motion in a few memorable phrases. It should remain in the judge's head and become the water-cooler line repeated between judges and clerks as they deliberate. Themes predict the issue the judge will struggle with.

Consider these examples of themes:

- On a motion for preliminary injunction: "A trade secret lost is lost forever."[1]

- Before the U.S. Supreme Court on a case testing the boundaries of the First Amendment: "We are talking about a funeral. If context is ever going to matter, it has to matter in the context of a funeral. Mr. Snyder simply wanted to bury his son in a private dignified manner."[2]

- In a child abuse case: "This case is about a mother's love. Her love of cocaine and herself."

---

1. *FMC Corp. v. Taiwan Tainan Giant Indus. Co.*, 730 F.2d 61, 63 (2d Cir. 1984).
2. *Snyder v. Phelps*, 562 U.S. 443 (2011).

- On a summary judgment motion in a patent infringement case: "They may as well have handed our product to the manufacturer and said, 'Here, make one for us.'"[3]

There is no reason to umbrella your entire case under one theme. Sub-themes are permissible and often advisable. Multiple themes work particularly well in a complicated matter such as a *Markman* hearing, multidistrict litigation (MDL), or class action, but also in the simpler cases with more than one facet.

As an example, in a motion to set aside a default judgment, the overarching theme may be, "Every person deserves his day in court." However, we know that Federal Rule of Civil Procedure 60(b) requires more than the platitude that every person deserves his day in court. It requires that there be excusable neglect on the part of the defendant in not answering the complaint. So a subtheme may be, "An attorney's neglect should not be visited on his unwary client."

Themes can also be created for fallback positions. If you see that a judge will not agree with you on your main theme, have alternative themes prepared and ready. For example, you start with a theme in a whistleblower case: "Mr. Doe is being punished for cooperating." As the motion develops, you see that the judge is completely unsympathetic toward Mr. Doe, and you decide to shift focus to the company. "The company should take responsibility for its faulty research."

3.2   The *Why*

Why use a theme in a motion hearing? First, the act of disciplined simplification helps to focus your thinking. Not only does it focus your thinking, but it focuses the judge's attention on what you see as important, gives her a framework to look at the case, and simplifies difficult concepts.

Second, getting immediately to the point will be well received by the court. Judges feel overburdened by their caseload and have little patience with attorneys who do not get to the core of the argument immediately. The detailed, foundation-building argument should have taken place through the papering of the motion. The motion is a chance to boil it down and highlight issues. It is a chance to discuss the issues with the judge. Themes help you simplify so you can discuss the issues efficiently.

Third, a theme straightaway captures a judge's attention, and with a captured audience you have a greater chance to keep the audience interested—at least for a while. A properly crafted theme is memorable. It can be replayed without struggle—"Sanctions should be a last resort option," for example. This theme insinuates

---

3. *Stryker Corp. v. Zimmer, Inc.*, 782 F.3d 649 (Fed. Cir. 2014).

that the moving party is premature and dramatic. It calls for reason and fairness, without whining for them.

Fourth, in communications, the rule of primacy and recency holds that a listener remembers what is said first and last in a presentation. If your first words are the essence of the case, then the judge will remember what you think is the crux of your case. It is imperative that you resound the theme throughout the motion. Start and finish with the theme, developing it as needed based on the reaction of the judge.

Fifth, a clever theme will reverberate in a judge's head well after the argument, and if it is *your* theme resonating, you are more likely to prevail. Resonating themes are also discussed among court staff. The theme may even end up in the opinion. A judge's life is boring, at least on the bench. Add a little fun to it with a theme, and you will be remembered.

3.3   The *How*

Begin by thinking about the underlying principles behind your motion. Many motions are rule driven, so the theory derives from a rule. Generic themes for common motions include the following.

MOTION	MOVANT'S THEMES	RESPONDENT'S THEMES
Motion to Dismiss	• Taking the allegations together still does not add up to a claim.	• We have pled enough. Sufficient notice has been given.
Motion for Summary Judgment	• The facts are so clear we can only get to one result.	• There only needs to be one factual dispute. Let me count the ways.
Motion to Compel Discovery	• Discovery rules are broad. This all can be sorted out in a motion in limine.	• What is being asked for is overly broad. Discovery is bound by the notion of proportionality. The request is burdensome.
Motions in Limine (exclude)	• This is context driven. Educate the judge on what will happen at trial if this comes in.	• Let's see what happens at trial. Indicate to the judge you need a context.
Motions for Sanctions	• The process is important and the court needs to gain control of it.	• Sanctions are unduly harsh, considering the circumstances.

MOTION	MOVANT'S THEMES	RESPONDENT'S THEMES
Motion for Interlocutory Appeals	• Scare the judge. • If this is not fixed now, then there is a bigger problem later. • If we are right, then we will have wasted an incredible amount of time and resources for naught. • We do not want to hold up the proceedings, but neither do we wish to duplicate efforts.	• Argue the merits. • The court was right. • Granting the request will result in piecemeal litigation. • If every ruling is taken up midstream, then chaos will result. • Balance is important.
Motion to Stay	• Judicial economy and fairness compel a stay. We are willing to compromise on the conditions for the stay. Suggest reasonable conditions.	• This is only a delay tactic. More time will accomplish nothing.
Post-trial motions	• You did not mean to make a mistake, but you did. • Mistakes happen.	• The decision was correct in the first place. • Do not second-guess a good decision.

Once you decide on a fitting generic theory, now create a memorable theme that personalizes your argument. You will find that often a broad theory effortlessly turns into a memorable theme. Be creative. Inspiration can come from many sources.

TECHNIQUE	DESCRIPTION	THEME EXAMPLES
Headline	Create a newspaper headline about your case. What would the headline or bumper sticker read?	• "Procedures aren't technical: they are foundational." • "Procedures ensure fairness." • "Hiding the ball prolongs litigation." (Discovery dispute) • "It's time to put up or shut up." (Summary judgment)
Legal sayings	Legal maxims that have survived the test of time.	• "Justice delayed is justice denied." (Laches motion) • "Equity does not help those with unclean hands." (Defense of a restraining order) • "Ignorance of the law is no excuse." (Prosecution of a contempt action) • "No person is above the law." (Contempt)

TECHNIQUE	DESCRIPTION	THEME EXAMPLES
Quotes from cases	Pick critical language that cannot be ignored and use it as your theme. Especially helpful to use with a judge who wants to be affirmed on appeal.	• "We are here to get rid of the clutter."[4] • "There is reasonable suspicion to stop." (Motion to suppress)[5]
Other side's words	Turn the other side's words from their papers into your theme.	• "We value judicial efficiency as much as the defendants." (Defending motion for interlocutory appeal or prosecution of a preliminary injunction)
Quotations or idioms	Quotes from books or on the internet	• "They are trying to make something out of nothing." (Summary judgment) • "Much ado about nothing." • "My client has never had a problem with drugs. He has had problems with the police."[6] (Motion to suppress) • "This is the second bite at the apple." (Claim/issue preclusion) • "The plaintiff is opening up Pandora's box." • "Some circumstantial evidence is very strong, as when you find a trout in the milk."[7] (Summary judgment) • "The defendant is acting like 'a tornado in a teapot.'"[8] (Defending motion for sanctions)
Advertisements	Ads are so well-known to wide audience they provide common material for themes.	• "'It's the real thing.'"[9] (Patent infringement) • "'Where's the beef?' There is no scientific basis for this."[10] (Excluding expert testimony)

4. *Heller Fin., Inc. v. Midwhey Powder Co., Inc.*, 883 F.2d 1286, 1294 (7th Cir. 1989).

5. *Terry v. Ohio*, 392 U.S. 1 (1967).

6. Paraphrasing Keith Richards.

7. Henry David Thoreau.

8. OKLAHOMA!, (Magna Theater Corp. 1955).

9. Coca-Cola Advertisement, 1969.

10. Wendy's Advertisement, 1984.

TECHNIQUE	DESCRIPTION	THEME EXAMPLES
Songs or poems	Find songs of the judge's generation to make your point.	• "'You don't need a weatherman to know which way the wind blows.'"[11] (Expert opinion is not helpful) • "'When you ain't got nothing, you got nothing to lose.'"[12] (Plaintiffs have no standing to complain)
Rhetorical questions	Ask a question, but be sure to answer the question.	• "Is there a material issue of fact? Yes, there are at least four of them." (Summary judgment) • "Where are the safeguards? There are none." (exclusion of evidence)
Metaphors	Comparing one thing to another simplifies complicated concepts.	• "It's fruit of a poisonous tree." (Motion to suppress) • "Level the playing field." • "Time is money."[13]
Rule of three	There is something magical about the rule of threes ("The Father, the Son, and the Holy Ghost." "Beginning, middle, and end." "See no evil, speak no evil, hear no evil." "Never have so few given so much to so many.") They are memorable and can provide a structure to your argument.	• "This case is about precedent, policy, and predictability." • "They are asking too much, with too little value, at too high a cost." (Discovery dispute)
Clichés (+)	While clichés can be annoying ("This is a fishing expedition."), they often provide a quick way to brainstorm the right theme. Start with a tired cliché, and then dress it up or change it to be fresh and more unexpected.	• "The plaintiff has cast its net too wide." • Alternative to "slippery slope": "Slip slidin' away."[14]

---

11. See Alex Long, *The Freewheelin' Judiciary: A Bob Dylan Anthology*, 38 Fordham Urb. L.J. 1363 (2011), for an interesting discussion of opinions where judges cite song lyrics.

12. *Id.* (citing Chief Justice Roberts' majority opinion in *Spring Communication Co. v. APCC Services*, 555 U.S. 269 (2008)).

13. See George Lakoff and Mark Johnson, *Metaphors We Live By* (Chicago: University of Chicago Press, 2003), for an innovative look at how humans think in metaphors.

14. PAUL SIMON, *Slip Slidin' Away*, on GREATEST HITS, ETC. (Columbia Records 1977).

Here are examples of the kind of themes that do not work:

TECHNIQUE	DESCRIPTION	BAD THEME EXAMPLES
Issue restatements	The judge knows this. You are wasting your time and the court's time. Say something the court does not know.	• "We are here for the court to decide whether to grant summary judgment."
Name calling	With the name calling, the judge knows she is ready to watch a mudslinging contest. Everyone gets dirty in the process.	• "Counsel is being disingenuous." • "There she goes again with the same faulty arguments." • "She is misleading the court."
Hyperbole	Exaggeration damages your credibility immediately. Once lost, credibility is difficult to regain. If the case is so obvious or clear, the judge is asking why are you here.	• "This is a simple case." • "The other side is clearly wrong." • "The answer is obvious."
Too cute by half	If the theme is too provocative, it becomes the subject of the discussion at the hearing.	• "The defense is 'runnin' against the wind.'"[15] (Motion to suppress on a fleeing charge) • "If we can't regulate the sale of broccoli, then we can't regulate health care."[16]
Clichés	Triteness does not inspire any judge and causes lost attention.	• "Justice is blind."
Easy to turn	Do not use a theme the other side can turn to their use.	• Case-dependent. As an example, if you leave a theme too open, the other side can use it against you. "Risk is part of life," used by defendant's counsel in a medical malpractice case could open wide a slew of comebacks from plaintiff's counsel, such as, "Yes, life is risky, Your Honor. But I doubt my client would have taken the risk of ingesting poison, had she known."
More than three sentences in length	The theme is a hook, not a dissertation.	• "We have tried to negotiate with the other side, but they continue to throw roadblocks in our way. The defense will not budge on the dollar amount, and they won't consider a more creative settlement offer, blah, blah, blah . . . ."

---

15. BOB SEGER, Against the Wind, on NINE TONIGHT (Capitol Records 1981).
16. A theme that was not used in *National Federation of Independent Business v. Sebelius*, 132 S.Ct. 2566 (2012).

3.4 What Do You Do with It?

Use your theme to capture the attention of the court immediately. Do not bury your lede. Your theme should come during the first seconds of your argument. After your succinct, memorable theme, explain the broader theme.

Repetition is a successful persuasion technique, so thread your theme throughout the argument. After you answer a judge's question, use your theme to bring the court back to the strengths of your case.

Themes can be like a refrain in a song: they provide comfort and bring the listener back to the main point. But sometimes, if used too frequently, a repetitive theme can become annoying. Avoid theme-rot by pivoting before your theme has become its own cliché.

Revive your stale theme with elegant repetition. Find other ways of saying your theme. Sometimes, this is accomplished by changing the words of the themes by using synonymous phrases.

- "Hiding the ball prolongs litigation."
- "Not providing discovery wastes everyone's time."
- "At this rate, we will never resolve the real issues."
- "The more arguing over these minor matters, the more the court's time is chewed up."
- "This is not a game of hide 'n seek."

Or, as another example:

- "There are six requirements, and the government has met each and every one."
- "The government covered all six requirements."
- "The law requires six things, and all six were satisfied."

Other times, try changing the delivery of the same theme. For example, you can put heavy stress on certain words:

"There are *six* requirements, and the government has met *each* and *every one*."

You can also slow down certain groups of words:

"*There are six requirements*, and the government has met each and every one."

Finally, you can show emotion in your voice by raising your pitch or volume through a section:

"There are six requirements, and the government *has met each and every one.*"

Themes help to convince a judge of the rightfulness of your cause. So too do facts. Once you craft a memorable theme, it is time to focus on the facts. Weave them together with the law, and you have high hopes for a promising ruling.

CHAPTER FOUR

FACTS

Let us begin by addressing the elephant in the room, the number-one question asked about discussing facts during a motion hearing: *Should you even talk about them?* After all, the facts are described in the pleadings and presumably the court has read them. And besides, judges often dismiss attorneys during their fact recitation with, "I know the facts, counsel. Proceed."

Facts must be a part of your motion argument. Facts matter. Facts are persuasive. Facts drive decisions.[1] Facts tell us who wins or who loses. Facts are also subject to interpretation. You want the judge to view the facts through your prism—to place your spin on what occurred and why.

Not talking about the facts during the hearing is like not talking about the facts to jurors during a closing argument. But at least with jurors, you know they have heard the facts during testimony and foreshadowed during the opening statement. With a judge, however, you never can be sure that he has read the papers in advance—and you certainly do not want to be so impertinent as to ask the judge if he has read them.

You are the expert of the facts, not the court. *You* have lived with your client's cause; the judge has not. *You* have interviewed your client and the witnesses, attended depositions, seen the documents and exhibits supporting your client's position; the judge has not. A persuasive presentation of the facts is vital to the success of any motion.

Look at any well-written appellate decision. After reading the facts, you should know who wins. You may not know until you have read the decision in its entirety *why* the party wins, but you will know *who* wins. Let us look at Justice Elena Kagan's recitation of the facts in *Miller v. Alabama.*[2] Evan Miller received a mandatory sentence of life without parole. The issue was whether a mandatory sentence of life without parole for a juvenile offender violated the Eighth Amendment's prohibition against cruel and unusual punishment. Justice Kagan recites the facts as follows:

> Evan Miller was 14 years old at the time of his crime. Miller had by
> then been in and out of foster care because his mother suffered from

---

1. Louis Brandeis, later an Associate Justice on the United States Supreme Court, is known for writing the Brandeis Brief that consisted of 100 pages—ninety-eight pages devoted to the facts and two pages to the law.
2. *Miller v. Alabama*, 132 S. Ct. 2455 (2012).

alcoholism and drug addiction and his stepfather abused him. Miller, too, regularly used drugs and alcohol; and he had attempted suicide four times, the first when he was six years old.

One night in 2003, Miller was at home with a friend, Colby Smith, when a neighbor, Cole Cannon, came to make a drug deal with Miller's mother. The two boys followed Cannon back to his trailer, where all three smoked marijuana and played drinking games. When Cannon passed out, Miller stole his wallet, splitting about $300 with Smith. Miller then tried to put the wallet back in Cannon's pocket, but Cannon awoke and grabbed Miller by the throat. Smith hit Cannon with a nearby baseball bat, and once released, Miller grabbed the bat and repeatedly struck Cannon with it. Miller placed a sheet over Cannon's head, told him "'I am God, I've come to take your life,'" and delivered one more blow. The boys then retreated to Miller's trailer, but soon decided to return to Cannon's to cover up evidence of their crime. Once there, they lit two fires. Cannon eventually died from his injuries and smoke inhalation . . . .

Relying in significant part on testimony from Smith, who had pleaded to a lesser offense, a jury found Miller guilty. He was therefore sentenced to life without the possibility of parole.

Did fourteen-year-old Miller win his appeal? Of course. Why did Justice Kagan introduce Miller as a fourteen-year-old who was in and out of foster homes because of his addicted mother and abusive stepfather? Before we learn of Miller's crime, why are we told that Miller attempted suicide four times, the first at age six? We know why. Facts drive the justice of the case. Facts convince us why fairness lies with one party or another. We know from reading the Justice's delivery of the facts that imposition of a mandatory life sentence on Miller would be unjust.

During your preparation, you created a factual theory. The factual theory explained why the facts compelled a result for you. This chapter offers techniques to persuasively present your facts to the court during the motion hearing so that the court will want to decide for your client.

Exercise

Read trial court or appellate court opinions. Begin with the facts. After reading the facts but before the analysis, try to decide who won. Consider what facts brought you to your conclusion, and then check to see if you guessed correctly.

4.1 Context before Facts

Give context for the facts before you recite them. In other words, do not start out your argument with "The facts of the case are . . . ." Chances are, if you begin your presentation this way, the judge will stop you. Instead, tell the court why the facts are important before reciting them. For example, "Mr. Blackburn drove home safely and followed every rule of road. The police officer had no reasonable suspicion to stop him and no probable cause to search his car." Telling the court upfront allows the court to understand the facts in the context of the issue. Otherwise, the judge is asking himself, "Why is this important? Why are you telling me this?"

4.2 Facts, Not Conclusions

Facts are convincing; conclusions are not. We can see facts, but cannot see conclusions. Facts lead a judge to his own conclusion. No judge likes to be forced into a corner. To persuade the judge, lead him to agree with the facts you develop. Keep to the facts, not conclusions.

Imagine you are at a hearing asking the court to compel discovery in a case. You argue that the defense has been dilatory in its responses. What does that mean? As a conclusion, the meaning is subjective to the listener. What is dilatory to one person may not be dilatory to another. Instead, set out the facts:

> Your Honor, we asked the other side for these documents six months ago. They were due five months ago. We did not receive them. So I called opposing counsel. He said I would receive them in one week. I did not receive them in a week, so the next week I wrote a letter to him again asking for the documents. I heard nothing. I called again. Still nothing. One month later, I filed this motion to compel discovery. Still nothing. Five months after these documents were due, and after repeated attempts to receive these documents, still nothing.

These facts can be seen by the judge. You are not merely moaning in a conclusory manner that you have been stonewalled by opposing counsel. The details convince the judge.

4.3 Coulda, Woulda, Shoulda

Facts include what did occur as well as what did not occur. Think about what could have or should have been done, but did not happen. Once you think through the possible choices that were not made, point them out.

Take this simple discovery dispute as an example:

> Your Honor, the court ordered discovery to be completed on June 1. I sent a set of interrogatories and a request for production of documents

to opposing counsel on January 1. They were due by February 28. I talked to opposing counsel on the phone two weeks later. He told me I would have the responses the next week. The next week came and he could have called me to tell me he couldn't make the deadline. He didn't, so I wrote a letter asking again for his responses. He could have answered my letter by phone explaining his problem with complying. He didn't. He could have written me a letter. He didn't. He could have told me he needed another thirty days to respond and I would have had no objection. He didn't. He could have told me his administrative assistant was sick and I would have understood. He didn't. He could have told me his dog ate the documents and I would have extended his deadline. He didn't.[3] He could have asked to have the discovery schedule changed by agreement. He didn't.

This tactic requires the creative genius of the attorney and can be used in many types of motion hearing. In a motion-to-dismiss hearing for failure to state a claim upon which relief can be granted, you can list all the facts that were not alleged in the complaint. In a *Daubert* hearing, specify all that an expert could have done, but did not. Did the expert conduct his own investigation, or rely on the raw data of another? What test did the expert use, and not use? In a motion to suppress evidence in a criminal case, what could, or should, the police have done but did not? Did the police talk to this witness, or that? Did the police take fingerprints, record a confession, or send the samples for analysis? In your motion to dismiss for lack of personal jurisdiction, specify the contacts the company did not have with the state.

Search for the omissions. What is missing is many times as important as what is there. Include those crucial omissions in your factual analysis.

4.4   Crucial Facts Only

Distill the facts to the crucial facts relevant to the motion. Tell the story of your motion and not the story of your case. Delete facts that are not important. Be picky; do not dump data on the court. Otherwise, the important facts of the motion are lost in a morass of irrelevant facts. You have only limited time before the court, so use it wisely. Otherwise, the judge will become disinterested—or worse, aggravated.

Decide what facts are crucial by doing the good-fact/bad-fact analysis we discussed in Chapter One. After you have brainstormed all the facts, good and bad, then decide which facts are essential. With each fact on your table of facts, ask yourself, "Is this necessary for the court to know to resolve this motion?" Your presentation should include both the crucial good facts and bad facts *relevant to the motion.*

---

3. Okay, kidding. But sometimes adding a slight, sarcastic bit of humor is a better way to register your complaint about opposing counsel than to adopt a whiny tone.

You may be tempted to include unrelated facts that engender sympathy for your client. Proceed with caution. Overtly appealing to a judge's sympathy seldom works. Obvious, blatant, and open appeals to emotions may backfire. However, we do know that judges are human beings who are affected by the emotions of a situation. A light sprinkle of emotional facts may be appropriate.

For example, suppose you represent the plaintiff in a negligence case and are arguing against a motion for summary judgment. The issue is duty, but your client was seriously injured in the accident. A brief mention that your client is paralyzed will suffice. A judge does not need to be told repeatedly that your client was seriously injured; he understands. Talking about your client's injuries any more risks aggravating the judge and potentially hurting your cause. Judges pride themselves on making logical decisions. Of course, sympathy and fairness factor into a judge's decisions, but clear attempts to appeal to a judge's emotions usually tell him your legal argument is weak.

Generally, the more dramatic the facts are, the fewer of them you need and the less emotion you need to inject during delivery. An advocate needs to carefully choose facts when describing a gruesome murder and deliver those selective facts without much emotion. The more intense and dramatic the facts are, the less dramatic you should be. That said, you may need to dress up your facts and dial up the emotion discussing a corporation's S Corp tax status or the employee benefit dispute within a complicated corporate takeover, or the judge will suffer.

Another common mistake is to delineate every date of every event. Do not start your sentences with the default that "on such and such date, this occurred . . . ." Except for certain motions, such as motions to dismiss because the action was not filed within the statute of limitations or speedy trial motions, dates are not important. Do not clutter the judge's mind with unnecessary dates. Doing so sends the judge's mind down a path of irrelevancy. He begins to think that the dates are the important facts to remember. Instead, focus on the sequential relationships: what events came first, second, and third. And do the math for the judge to drive home your points. Instead of saying that on June 24 a default judgment was entered and the following year on February 23 a motion to set aside the default was filed, tell the court it was almost eight months after the default judgment before the motion to set aside was filed.

Too many facts are problematic, but so are too few facts. The danger of knowing too much is that you assume the judge shares that knowledge; as a result, you have a tendency to start the story of your motion in the middle. If the judge is not confident, she is unlikely to ask you to backpedal. If the judge does not stop you for clarification, then you have lost the judge. To avoid this, tell your story to someone who has never heard it to ensure that you have not omitted necessary facts. Follow the Goldilocks principle of facts: not too many, not too few, just right.

Consider a motion for summary judgment. Imagine you represent a local restaurant, Planet Burger. John Smith sues the restaurant for negligence for breaching its duty of care to its customers. One customer was killed and five were injured, including Smith, when a truck owned by Kenneth Levy crashed through the window of the restaurant. Levy also died in the accident. You filed a motion for summary judgment on Planet Burger's behalf alleging that it owed no duty to the plaintiffs because Levy's actions were not reasonably foreseeable.

This story of the motion gives, quite simply, too many facts:

> *Counsel*: Planet Burger is a wholly owned subsidiary of Partial Foods Inc. Planet Burger was incorporated in 2012. Partial Foods purchased the restaurant premises on July 20, 2012, and rented it to Planet Burger soon thereafter on July 31, 2013. The organic meat restaurant is on the corner of Western and Chicago Avenues in Chicago in the up-and-coming and trendy Ukrainian Village. The restaurant is positioned nine feet from the west side of Western Avenue and nine feet from the north side of Chicago Avenue. Between the curb and the windows of the restaurant is a three-foot-wide ditch that is two feet deep, a five-foot-wide sidewalk, and a one-foot-wide grassy area. On both Western and Chicago Avenues, the restaurant's façade is entirely covered with picture windows. Inside the restaurant, tables abut the windows so that the patron may view the city landscape while eating.
>
> On September 25, 2015, at 2:00 a.m., immediately before closing time, six patrons were sitting in booths facing Chicago Avenue.
>
> Meanwhile, Kenneth Levy had a fight with his wife at his home at Rockwell Street and Chicago Avenue, which was three blocks away, and left in his 2012 Dodge Charger traveling east down Chicago Avenue. Before he got into his car, Levy had drunk a twelve-pack of beer in the preceding three hours. Their fight was about his frequent drunkenness.
>
> As Levy drove down Chicago Avenue at 45 miles per hour—20 miles per hour over the speed limit—he crossed the centerline of Chicago Avenue immediately before Western Avenue and, at exactly 2:05 a.m., crashed into the picture window facing Chicago Avenue. Jenny West died, as did Levy, before the emergency crew arrived. The other five patrons received multiple injuries: Clive Gentry, a broken leg; Paul Bayou, a fractured pelvis; and Kathy Kite, Mandy Lopez, and Henry Aster, minor cuts and bruising.
>
> Levy's autopsy revealed a blood alcohol content of .18. Levy had no insurance, so all the patrons sued Planet Burger for negligence alleging that Planet Burger breached its duty of care to them.

This version of the facts wastes time on facts that are unimportant to the question of whether Planet Burger could have reasonably foreseen the accident. It sends the judge on a wild-goose chase through irrelevant matters, such as the relationship between Planet Burger and Partial Foods, Inc.; the dates of incorporation; the dates of purchase of the restaurant; and the injuries sustained by the plaintiffs. These diversions take the court's focus off the main issue, weakening the argument.

Now let's look at sample language with the opposite problem: it divulges too *few* facts.

> *Counsel*: Planet Burger had no duty to the customers of its restaurant. Levy was drunk when he crashed into the restaurant windows, causing the plaintiff's injuries. He was speeding. There is no way that Planet Burger could have foreseen Levy's actions.

This rendition of the facts leaves the listener wondering if she came into a story already in progress. Perhaps the judge read the papers before the hearing, but perhaps not. Even so, with a busy docket that day, the judge may not remember the facts of this motion. Counsel assumes the court knows as much about the case as she does. In addition, the skeletal facts fail to paint a picture for the judge that he can remember.

Just as Goldilocks discovered at the house of the three bears, there is a happy medium for you. Not too many facts, not too few . . . just right:

> *Counsel*: Planet Burger could not have reasonably foreseen that the drunken Kenneth Levy would crash into its building, killing Jenny West and injuring its other customers. Planet Burger is at the corner of Western and Chicago Avenues in Chicago. Here is a diagram of how the restaurant is situated at that corner [*showing a map of the location*]. You can see the restaurant is built on the set-back lines, complying with city ordinance. Planet Burger stays open until 2:00 a.m. every night or until the last customer leaves.
>
> September 25 of last year, at 2:00 a.m., it was a busy night at Planet Burger. The six plaintiffs were sitting at booths immediately next to the windows of the restaurant overlooking Chicago Avenue, when Levy, after fighting with his wife and drinking twelve cans of beer, got behind the wheel of his car, drove eastbound on Chicago Avenue, crossed the center line, went across the westbound lane, jumped the curb, sped across the sidewalk, hopped a three-foot-wide ditch, and crashed through the window, killing one plaintiff and injuring the others. Levy was driving 20 miles per hour over the speed limit, with a blood alcohol content of .18, which is over twice the legal limit. Levy died as a result of the crash, with no insurance coverage. The plaintiffs sued Planet Burger for negligence. Planet Burger could not have foreseen the actions of Levy and thus had no duty to the plaintiffs.

Note that although the "just right" version of the facts has fewer facts than the "too much" version, the "just right" version contains additional facts crucial to the issue of foreseeability. For example, included in the facts are that the restaurant was in compliance with local set-back requirements and that Levy went across the westbound lane, jumped the curb, hopped a ditch, and sped across the sidewalk, before crashing into the restaurant.

> **Exercise**
>
> For every case, practice both zeroing in on the facts and staying broad. Do this once a month. To zero in on the facts, set a three-minute timer for yourself and describe the facts in detail. To stay broad, re-tell the same set of facts in thirty seconds and force yourself to select the key facts. Audio-record yourself and listen for extraneous facts and ways you can summarize the facts.

4.5 Reasonable Inferences

Stick with the facts in a motion hearing, but that does not mean you cannot make reasonable inferences from the facts. You can, and must, connect the dots for the judge.

For example, in a discovery dispute, if the opposing counsel refuses to provide discovery, argue that the court can infer from his conduct that disclosure hurts his case. If a complaint alleging fraud omits that the plaintiff reasonably relied on the defendant's misrepresentation, then at a hearing on a motion to dismiss, argue that the reasonable inference is that the plaintiff cannot prove reliance. Make the connection for the judge.

4.6 Bad Facts

Some lawyers work very hard to bury bad facts, and yet the bad news always finds a way to be heard. Include the bad facts in your presentation. If you own them, you can spin and minimize them. If you do not, you look afraid of those facts and will lose your credibility. Your case's credibility is also at risk if you do not explain bad facts from your vantage point.

Your bad facts must come from your mouth. Otherwise, they gain increased importance when they come from the other side. If you do not deal with them, the judge will believe that you cannot. Do not dwell on them; however, include them in your factual presentation. Spend at least three times as much time talking about your good facts than your bad ones. Exceptions do exist, especially for the respondent in a motion who has to tackle the hard issues out of the gate. In general, place bad facts in the middle of your story, surrounded by your good facts.

By way of illustration, assume that counsel represents Jose Lopez, who is charged with possession of a benzodiazepine without a valid prescription. Lopez was stopped on the interstate because he was speeding. Counsel filed a motion to suppress the pills found in a pill case in a duffel bag in the back seat of the car, claiming Lopez was the victim of profiling. In his police report, the officer states that he searched Lopez's car because Lopez was sweating and engaged in "furtive" behavior.

> *Counsel*: Jose's car was searched because the officer said Jose was sweating and engaging in furtive behavior. What is furtive behavior anyway? We don't know because the officer does not explain it in his report. And sweating. Of course he was sweating: the police had stopped him. Most of us are uncomfortable when stopped by the police. Jose was driving to his mother's home after receiving a call from her that she had fallen. The officer was looking for drug dealers.

By putting the bad fact upfront—the furtive behavior—counsel gives credibility to the government's position. Counsel is implicitly saying that Jose's furtive behavior is so important that he must talk about it first. Rather, he should lead with his good facts. Also, the above advocate spent most of his time talking about his bad facts and simply tacked on the good facts at the end.

Now examine how counsel can de-emphasize those bad facts.

> *Counsel*: There was no probable cause to search Jose's car. Jose has never been stopped by the police or arrested. He has worked for five years at Menards, stocking shelves. On the day of his arrest, he received a phone call from his mother. She told him that she had fallen and needed his help. Worried about his elderly mother, Jose immediately got in his car and headed on I-94 to his mother.
>
> In the meantime, Officer Gray was on duty with the Drug Enforcement Task Force driving on I-94. I-94 is a corridor known by the police to be used to transport drugs from Detroit to Chicago. Officer Gray was looking for drug dealers.
>
> Officer Gray saw a Hispanic male, twenty-five years of age, going ten miles over the speed limit. The officer stopped him. Jose was nervous about his mom and being pulled over, so it is understandable why he was sweating. By all accounts, Jose gave Officer Gray his valid driver's license and waited patiently in the car while Officer Gray wrote him a ticket. When the officer handed the ticket to Jose, he asked him to step out of the car and began to search the car. The officer claims that he searched Jose's car because Jose was sweating and "engaged in furtive behavior." What is furtive behavior? Even the officer in his report does not designate what it is. The officer was looking for drug dealers and Jose fit the cultural profile of a typical drug dealer. That's why Jose was stopped.

This version of the facts explains the defendant's behavior only after painting a favorable picture of Jose for the court. Note also that much more time was spent on the good facts, as opposed to the bad.

4.7   Overstating the Facts

Do not exaggerate the facts of your case. Your opponent will be sure to let the judge know you are overstating. As a result, the judge will question the strength of your case, because attorneys with strong cases do not need to overstate. Most importantly, though, you will lose the trust of the judge.

4.8   Word Choice

Use plain English—simple words that clearly and succinctly convey your meaning. So use "cars," not "vehicles;" "deals," not "transactions;" "before," not "prior to;" "contracts," not "documents;" "sign," not "execute;" "home," not "residence;" "ask," not "inquire;" and the list goes on.

Use words that create pictures in the mind of the judge. "Car" not only is a simpler word than "vehicle," but it conveys an image. A vehicle could be a tractor, semi-truck, motorcycle, or car. Tom Singer, a trial attorney, longtime professor of trial advocacy at Notre Dame Law School, and lover of poetry, uses a story about President Franklin D. Roosevelt to make the point that words should be simple. During World War II, FDR was given a placard to place in over a thousand federal offices. The placard said: "It is obligatory to extinguish all illumination before leaving the premises." FDR's response? "Why the hell can't we just say 'Put out the lights when you leave'?"[4]

4.9   Exhibits

Study after study confirms the old adage that a picture is a worth a thousand words. Sixty-five percent of the population learns visually, yet most communication in a courtroom is auditory. Visual aids increase understanding. Consider a case involving an automobile accident. To see a picture or diagram of where the accident occurred increases the judge's comprehension. Likewise, looking at a complaint to show its deficiencies assists the judge's understanding.

Visual aids also make facts more believable. It is one thing to say that a debt was paid in full and quite another to show the canceled check. Testifying about an agreement is less convincing than seeing and reading it. Visual aids stay with the judge.

Take advantage of such research: create and refer to exhibits to make your important points. When possible and appropriate, increase the court's understanding by using a visual aid. Maps, diagrams, tables, pictures, models, slideshows, depositions, or affidavit excerpts are all effective.

Some demonstratives will come from the papers you have submitted or witnesses you will call. Others, like slideshows or timelines, will summarize the evidence or

---

4. Lawrence S. Bartell, *True Stories of Strange Events and Odd People: A Memoir* (Bloomington, IN: iUniverse, 2014).

law. As a matter of courtesy and efficiency, make sure that you have extra copies for the court, opposing counsel, and witnesses.

Finally, when using the exhibit, use it to enhance, and not distract from, your presentation. Do not discuss an exhibit as the judge is rummaging to find it. Multitasking is difficult for all of us; judges are no different. Before continuing to speak, wait until the judge lets you know that he has found the exhibit and the portion you wish to discuss. Then orient him to the exhibit. Tell him what he is looking at before you highlight a specific portion of the exhibit. If the exhibit is a map, tell him what direction is north. If showing a picture of an accident scene, let him know that the picture was taken immediately after the accident, looking to the south, before you zero in on the skid marks. If it is a document, explain what it is before you turn to paragraph ten. In other words, let him get his bearings before you describe the particulars.

Here are examples of pictures of street scenes, in order from the most clear to the most confusing.

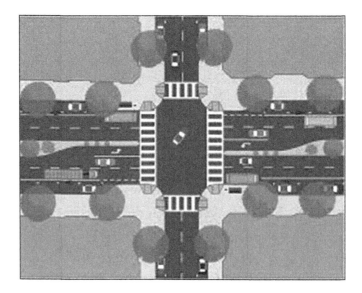

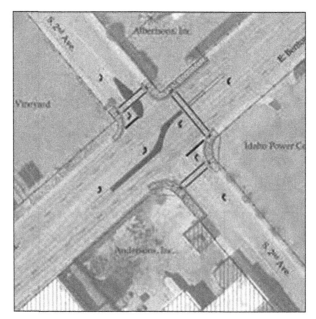

4.10 Creating Visual Pictures

You want the judge to remember your version of the facts of the case. This is the case regardless of whether the judge is taking the decision of your motion under advisement. You want a good image to stick. To make the memory of the facts of your case stay in the judge's mind, create visual pictures with your words.

In *Moonwalking with Einstein*,[5] Joshua Foer tells the story of how he rose to the finals of the USA Memory Championship. The competition requires the contestants to memorize the order of cards in two decks in five minutes. To perform this Herculean task, Foer assigned a person, place, or action to each card. So, the king of hearts may be Einstein, the eight of diamonds moonwalking, and the three of clubs the Louvre. If the above cards came up, Foer would create in his mind a picture of Einstein moonwalking in the Louvre. Through a series of visual images, he memorized both decks.

All of our brains are made to remember pictures. Judges' brains are too. Paint pictures in the judge's mind by using sensory language—language that helps the judge see, hear, feel, smell, touch, remember, and imagine. During a hearing on a motion to suppress the drugs found in your client's car, paint the picture of your client waiting on the berm of a busy expressway at rush hour in ninety-degree weather for half an hour until the drug dog arrives. Or, in the middle of discovery, paint the mental picture of thousands of banker's boxes of documents being scanned, digitized, and electronically filed, but a few boxes—those containing bad faith claims—are left on the side. These images will not be forgotten by the judge.

4.11 Creating the Story of Your Motion

Put your facts in a story. If you do not create the story, the judge will. People think in terms of stories. Stories have characters—some good and honorable, others evil and flawed. These characters have reasons why they act as they do.

Stories begin with the characters in a state of calm that is interrupted by trouble. The actors try to resolve the conflict, but cannot. An event occurs or a person swoops in to resolve the difficulty, bringing about a happily ever after. In the end, a moral lesson is learned by all.

Your motions, like all legal disputes, are stories about people. Your audience, the judge, will assign a hero and a villain to the story at hand, and make logical causal connections based on the facts you deliver. Present your motion so the judge reaches the conclusion that your side wears the white hat while the other side wears the black one. Avoid calling your client "plaintiff," "defendant," "petitioner," or "respondent." First, it is confusing to the court. The judge, with each reference, must remember who is who. Second, it dehumanizes your client. Your goal is to make your client likeable. Start by calling her by name and not calling her your "client." The term "client" emphasizes that you are a hired gun. After all, your relationship to her is not what is important; who she is, what she did, and why she acted as she did is what is important.

---

5. Joshua Foer, *Moonwalking with Einstein: The Art and Science of Remembering Everything* (New York: Penguin Press, 2011).

Dehumanize the other side, but do not do so by constantly calling them "defendant" or "respondent." This confuses the judge and is too blatant an attempt to demonize. Instead, call the opposing side by his full name: John Wayne Gacy, for example, or simply his last name, Gacy. Call the opponent by their full corporation name: Campbell Soup Corporation, Inc. or Allstate Fire and Casualty Insurance Corporation, Inc. But after that first time, shorten the name to a commonly used word or phrase—Campbell's or Allstate—so you do not get tongue-tied.

This is not to say you may not judiciously call the opposing party *plaintiff, defendant, petitioner,* or *respondent.* At times, the reference clarifies matters or strengthens your argument: "This is the twentieth discovery motion brought by the petitioner. Each and every time, this court has dismissed the motion. Here we are again."

Let us reexamine Justice Kagan's *Miller v. Alabama* opinion, discussed earlier in this chapter. We know that Miller struck Cannon repeatedly over the head with a baseball bat, causing his death. Yet, Justice Kagan humanizes Miller even while she recognizes his horrendous murder, softening the blow by giving us some context for his conduct.

Justice Kagan also artfully presents the facts so that the reader unconsciously makes a causal connection between Miller's neglected childhood and his act of murder. Making a causal connection between two events is a natural tendency. It could very well be that young Miller mutilated animals when he was four or committed any number of horrendous acts. But, because we hear only limited facts, we naturally connect those facts as cause and effect. If you do not provide the causal connection for the judge, he will do it himself—and it may not be the connection you want him to make.

In many cases, tell your story in chronological order. Usually, it is easier to follow a story, particularly for the first time, if it is told chronologically. However, stories may also be sequenced by describing the paths of two parties, whose paths then collide. For example, in a motion to suppress hearing, you might begin with the story of your client and his day, followed by the story of the overworked, irritated cop—with the two then meeting and the misunderstanding that resulted in your client's unlawful arrest.

Good stories begin with equilibrium, until trouble comes. The trouble may be from an outside source or from one of the actors. The cause of the trouble is generally the person who has the motive to cause it. Listeners to the story superimpose motives on the actors. Give enough of the facts to the judge so the judge will believe your version of the motives of the parties. Let us go back to our example in Chapter One. There, an insurance company refused to give to its insured documents showing bad faith claims filed against it. The insurance company did not digitize the records, although other records were automated. The insured wants the court to believe the records were not scanned because the insurance company has

Facts

a history of bad faith claims to hide. The insurance company wants the court to believe that its motive is purely financial and that the insured's motive is to force an unfair settlement. Both side's story must contain the facts that support their version of the parties' motivations.

All is well that ends well, and the judge writes the ending: the decision. All good endings have a moral lesson. Here, the message is either "A litigant cannot get away with hiding information" or "Asking for too much, with too little value, at too high a cost is unreasonable." You want *your* theme to become the moral lesson, which should be the reason the case matters to the judge.[6]

4.12 Speed Crafting

Be cognizant of the rate of your speed when delivering your facts. The rate of speed is the number of words per minute that you speak. Slow talkers speak at 145 words per minute or less, while fast talkers speak at 185 words or more per minute. Many people speak too quickly and need to slow down; far fewer are slow talkers and need to speed up. More speed techniques are discussed in Chapter Nine. But for now, know that variety of your speech rate keeps a listener interested. If you are consistently slow paced, the listener falls asleep. If you are consistently fast paced, the listener cannot keep up with you and loses interest. Variety maintains interest.

When delivering your facts, when should you slow down and when should you speed up your rate of speech? *Slow down* when you make your most important points. *Speed up* on less important points or when you wish to build momentum or show enthusiasm, passion, or conviction.

Return for a moment to the Planet Burger case in section 4.4, above. Here is a transcript of when counsel should slow down and speed up her delivery.

> [*Begin at a measured pace.*]
>
> Planet Burger could not have reasonably foreseen that the drunken Kenneth Levy would crash into its building, killing Jenny West and injuring its other customers.
>
> [*Pause.*]
>
> [*Quicker pace.*]
>
> Planet Burger is at the corner of Western and Chicago Avenues in Chicago. Here is a diagram of how the restaurant is situated at that corner.

---

6. For an extended discussion of storytelling, see Phillip N. Meyer's *Storytelling for Lawyers* (Oxford, United Kingdom: Oxford University Press, 2014).

Point Well Made   63

[*Pause, then a measured, regular pace.*]

You can see the restaurant is built on the set-back lines, complying with city ordinance [*showing map of location*].

[*Pick up the pace.*]

Planet Burger stays open until 2:00 a.m. each night or until the last customer leaves.

September 25 of last year, at 2:00 a.m., it was a busy night at Planet Burger. The six plaintiffs were sitting at booths immediately under the windows of the restaurant overlooking Chicago [*measured build in speed to make it sound like there were other out-of-control actions that led to this accident*], when Levy, after fighting with his wife and drinking twelve cans of beer, got behind the wheel of his car, drove eastbound on Chicago Avenue, crossed the center line, went across the westbound lane, jumped the curb, hopped a three-foot-wide ditch, sped across the sidewalk, and crashed through the window, killing one plaintiff and injuring the others.

[*Slow pace.*]

Levy was driving 20 miles per hour over the speed limit, with a blood alcohol content of .18, which is over twice the legal limit.

[*Pause. Deliver the next line at a medium pace.*]

Levy died as a result of the crash, with no insurance coverage. The plaintiffs sued Planet Burger for negligence.

[*Pause.*]

Planet Burger could not have foreseen the actions of Levy and thus had no duty to the plaintiffs.

Alternatively, to use the facts as a way for theme variation, slow down for the important information. The entire argument is that Planet Burger could not have reasonably foreseen Levy's actions. Slowly deliver the premise of the argument so that it will resonate with the judge. When the speaker begins to tell the judge about Levy's actions, the rate of speed should substantially slow down with a pause after each clause: "When Levy [*pause*], after fighting with his wife and drinking twelve cans of beer [*pause*], got behind the wheel of his car [*pause*], drove eastbound on Chicago Avenue [*pause*], crossed the center line [*pause*], went across the westbound lane [*pause*], hopped a three-foot-wide ditch [*pause*] . . . ." The slow cadence with pauses allows the court to digest the information, see Levy's actions, and realize there was nothing Planet Burger could have done to stop the accident.

Exercise

Practice telling the plot of a movie or TV show in thirty seconds, then in three minutes. Plan where you will slow down your rate of speed for emphasis, and where you will speed up to show enthusiasm and conviction. Time your deliveries. Once satisfied with your ability to manipulate speed effectively, switch topics to the facts of one of your cases.

Now that we have dissected two major components of an oral motion presentation—theme and facts—we turn to another key component: the law.

Chapter Five

The Law

A true show of brilliance happens when the most complicated legal matters are boiled down into simple sound bites. The law must support your legal theory, if not, acknowledge it and say why. When presenting the law, a good advocate discusses the current state of the law and the purpose behind the law. Sometimes a legal argument involves pushing a current legal theory one step further. A creative advocate clearly outlines what elements must be proven to win and who bears the burden of proof.

5.1 Keep It Simple

Keep your discussion of the law simple. Simple delivery should be clear and logical. A judge rarely accepts contradictory or circular legal positions. Complicated arguments require too much work for the listener. Once a judge has to fight to listen and pay attention, she shuts down.

A good judge may rightly use the power of her position to interrupt a convoluted advocate with questions. Sometimes, questions are a way for the judge to help unpack the attorney's argument into digestible chunks. This can be done overtly or subconsciously. The judge may realize that the advocate is weaving a complicated legal argument and stop him in his tracks to give him a chance to revise the delivery or to point out the advocate's error. Other times during an argument, the judge shows non-verbal signs of confusion, and eventually asks a series of questions, struggling to find logic in the advocate's legal theory. Either way, it is tough to resurrect an overly complicated legal theory. The back-and-forth question and answer that ensues takes time away from the only important issues at hand: the judge's concerns.

Some attorneys fight the advice to simplify a legal argument because they contend that the legal argument is indeed complicated. They keep fighting—and keep losing. Begin by simplifying foundational principles until you and the judge see eye to eye on each level before launching into the complicated argument. A judge knows that it takes time, creativity, and smarts to speak simply.

Sometimes finding the right way to discuss the law simply and powerfully is a challenge. When the spark of creativity is lacking, try spinning a legal theory into a delivery style with more structure. Sometimes the framework allows for creativity to flow. Here are some examples:

WAYS TO SIMPLIFY DIFFICULT CONCEPTS AND OTHER PERSUASIVE TECHNIQUES FOR DEALING WITH THE LAW		
Enumeration	Divide the substance into numbered sections. Keep the list to five or fewer divisions. Once a numbering system is established, stay faithful to that regime. Do not over-enumerate (i.e., no sub-numbering systems in oral delivery).	"There are three reasons why the law supports our side."
Step approach	Similar to enumeration, but here the numbered items build on one another.	"Now that we've satisfied the second prong of the regulation, we move to the third part of the test."
Compare and contrast	Compare and contrast the pros and cons, the risks and benefits, the plaintiff's and defendant's perspectives on an issue. Use this model to showcase similarities or differences between two things.	"The Ninth Circuit takes [x] position, while the Sixth Circuit takes the opposite view."
Lay foundations	Start with foundations and build upon them once an understanding is reached.	"Your Honor, it's long-standing Supreme Court precedent that defendants must be Mirandized. Let's talk about the nuance of whether an undocumented-immigrant defendant must be Mirandized."
Principle and application	Set up a legal principle and apply it to the facts in the present case or to the facts of a cited case.	"The First Amendment provides for freedom of speech. In the case of *Arizona v. Emperor*, the young boy's shouts during the parade were considered protected speech."
Repetition	Can be a word-for-word recitation of a line or message. Alternatively, repetition can be the recitation of synonymous phrases. This is one way to avoid the danger of the court losing interest, because of drumbeat repetition.	Early in the argument: "A likelihood of success on the merits must be shown." Later in the argument: "It doesn't look like the plaintiff could ultimately satisfy his burden, Your Honor."
Headline and recap	Tell the judge what you are going to say, explain it, and remind her of what you said. The headline signals to the judge that you are starting a new topic. An explanation would follow. The recap restates the meaning of the headline.	Headline: "The attorney-client privilege should be protected." Recap: "The default position should be to guard the privilege, not destroy it."

WAYS TO SIMPLIFY DIFFICULT CONCEPTS AND OTHER PERSUASIVE TECHNIQUES FOR DEALING WITH THE LAW		
Visuals	Prepare a foam board, PowerPoint, chart, table, or picture with any information that would be better understood visually.	• "Your Honor sees here the words of Justice Kennedy that control this case." • "The injuries seen here are worth millions, and we are entitled to know if the defendant has millions."
Sensory	Give examples so the judge can see the natural consequences of a principle or proposition. When giving examples, paint a picture for the judge that she will remember later. Use the senses when possible and/or scenario dialogue.	"Imagine someone going into an attorney's office for a first visit. They sit across one another at a small table, and the attorney says, 'Everything you say to me is confidential. Oh, except that the judge may review what you tell me today and what I advise you may not fall within the privilege.' What will that do to attorney–client communications?"

> **Exercise**
>
> Take one legal theory from a motion and spontaneously deliver it out loud, trying the different organizational options above. Keep the deliveries crisp. Decide what style best fits the particular legal theory.

5.2 But, Do Not Oversimplify

Imagine a spectrum of simple to complicated. It starts on the left, with an oversimplified argument, which offends the intellect of the judge. While it is true that the goal is simplicity, it is a balancing act and it should not be made *too* simple. If it does, then it sounds as if the advocate is talking down to the judge. The judge should not be left to think that the advocate thinks she is stupid. Needless to say, it is not a good persuasion technique. You run the risk of patronizing a judge if you oversimplify.

Oversimplified	Simple	Complicated

On the other side of the spectrum is the complicated argument, which causes confusion and/or lends itself to misinterpretation. You will lose your judge if you speak like an encyclopedia.

In the middle of the spectrum is the balanced, simple argument. If you find yourself on the oversimplified side, the legal theory needs to be more sophisticated. If you find yourself on the complicated side, the legal theory needs to be made more elegant, precise, and basic.

Example — Too Complicated

Counsel: Your Honor, the crime-fraud exception to the attorney–client privileged communications allows disclosure of communications in the furtherance of future illegal conduct. The exception applies when the client strategizes a fraudulent scheme when consulting an attorney's advice to further the stratagem.

Huh? Even the judge, familiar with the crime fraud exception, will find this explanation difficult to understand. Now let's turn to the overly simplistic argument that insults the judge's intelligence.

Example — Too Simple

Counsel: Your Honor, conversations between attorneys and their clients are confidential. This is called the attorney–client privilege. There is an exception to this rule. When a client seeks advice from an attorney to further the client's fraudulent plan or crime, then the conversations are not privileged. This is called the crime-fraud exception.

Duh, of course the court knows that attorney–client communications are confidential. And the judge also knows that the conversation is generally privileged. This simplicity risks the judge shutting off from listening to anything else this advocate says. A balanced approach simplifies, but not overly so.

Example — Simple, but Not Too Simple

Counsel: Your Honor, an exception to attorney–client privilege is the crime-fraud exception. When a client seeks advice from an attorney for the purposes of committing a future fraud or crime, the communication is not privileged. It does not matter what the attorney knows or does not know when providing the advice.

This example simply, clearly, and precisely explains the crime-fraud exception.

Exercise

Take one legal theory from a brief and draft three different ways to present the theory:

1) Oversimplified
2) Simplified
3) Complicated

5.3   Know the Law

If you cite a statute, rule, or regulation in your papers, be able to discuss what it is, what it means, and why you used it. Know the holding of each of the cases cited by you or your opponent and how the holding impacts your motion. Also, be acquainted with the facts of all cases cited in the papers. Know the facts well enough that you can distinguish the cases that hurt you and use the cases that help you. Plan how you will discuss the cases. Your discussion of a case changes, depending on whether it is good or bad for you and whether the facts are the same or different than yours.

GOOD CASES		BAD CASES	
Same facts, same holding	**Different facts, same holding**	**Different facts, different holding**	**Same facts, different holding**
Quote the cases, weave into the theme.	Use carefully; show comparisons and admit distinctions before your opponent does.	Distinguish facts, show how if the facts in that case were the same as the present facts, the holding would have been different.	Distinguish holding or how it was applied, argue public policy.

Before the argument, prepare brief talking points about the similarity of the facts to your case or the irrelevance of the dissimilarities. Take limited information about the cases to the podium with you. We will talk more about what to bring to the podium in Chapter Seven.

5.4   Use the Law Elegantly

Just because you are prepared to discuss all the cases cited does not mean you *should*. Be focused in your discussion of the law. Judges appreciate an attorney who sets out a legal principle and then applies the principle to the facts of the case. Many times, the legal principle has become a powerful "magic phrase" to be used and repeated throughout the hearing. These magic phrases encapsulate the legal holding or summarize the statute or regulation. The phrases become like comfortable shoes, easy for the judge to wear. If the judge is not comfortable with the phrase, then the succinct and memorable phrase should help in the education process. The repetition, either through exact quoting or synonymous phrasing, takes a once unfamiliar legal phrase to a familiar one for the judge.

Be discerning when discussing the case law. Use one or possibly two cases for each point you wish to make. Citing laundry lists of cases does not impress a judge; instead, it makes her think that the law is not settled—or worse, that you do not know the difference between important and minor cases. Pick your best case and hit it hard. Also, unless you are asked, do not get into the weeds of the case. If you do, you will chew up the limited time that you have. Set out the legal principles involved and apply them to the facts of your case.

If you decide to quote something from a case, do not misquote the law or take the case out of context. You immediately lose credibility, appear unintelligent, or open yourself up to an attack from opposing counsel. If you quote from a case where the holding cuts against your legal position, tell the court. Do not wait for opposing counsel to inform the judge. Be exact, even if you need to extrapolate your position from the exact words. You can use the exact words from the case or use similar or analogous language to return to your argument.

5.5 Argue the Purpose of or the Common Sense Reason Behind the Law

During your preparation, you identified the purpose or policy reasons behind the law. To create a convincing public-policy argument to persuade a judge to hold in your favor, ask yourself: What is the common-sense reason for the law? What policy implications does it advance? What is the reason behind the law that is in concert with our position? The preferred result should further the purpose of the rule.

Common-sense, public-policy arguments are compelling. Suppose you are arguing for sanctions to be imposed on the opposing party because he failed to respond to discovery. A convincing argument is that process matters and the rules allowing the court to impose sanctions are designed for the judge to manage the process. Without penalties, the offending party will continue to obstruct. A right without a remedy is no right.

A common-sense, public-policy argument can augment other arguments. Or a policy argument can be used when your underlying arguments are weak or non-existent. Argue that a ruling for you is consistent with the purpose and intent of the law. If you ask for a default judgment to be set aside, argue that the law and fairness favors resolving cases on the merits, particularly if a claim or defense has been barred. Or, if you represent a medical doctor who signed an overly restrictive non-compete agreement, argue that enforcing the contract as written is against public policy because a patient is always entitled to be treated by a medical doctor of his own choosing.

Intertwine public-policy arguments with an argument that the natural evolution of the law favors a ruling for you. Predict where the law is going by looking at how it has developed in the past. Use public-policy arguments if you want the court to extend the law. But, do not wait for the judge or opposing counsel to surprise you with a question revealing that your interpretation of the law is not the current state of the law. Instead, address it head on and urge the court to act consistent with public policy.

Example

Counsel: Your Honor, a progressive interpretation of the law is needed to prevent an injustice here. The case law here is old and does not account for the constant and rapidly changing landscape of modern cybersecurity. The law's purpose is to protect information and encourage companies to do the same. It is not intended to punish a company that gets hacked despite its best efforts to prevent an intrusion.

5.6 Practice Aloud

Figuring out whether you strike the right legal argument requires practicing aloud. Do not speak your legal theory aloud for the first time in front of the judge. A reader can digest more complicated material than a listener. A judge is also a reader. The written word gives a reading audience time to digest—and reread, if necessary. The judge is a prisoner to the speed and complexity chosen by the attorney. In preparation, an attorney has to talk about the legal theory out loud to hear whether it makes sense off the page. Your arguments will become clearer and more concise because you will hear the confusing sections and complicated words.

Today's technology affords attorneys the opportunity to practice out loud and hear an instant recording. If you do not have a phone with an audio-recording function, then invest in a portable recording device that will allow you to practice while you drive, exercise, or pace around your office. Set a timer and record the planned argument. Play it back and listen first for clarity and simplicity. Put yourself in the shoes of a judge who did not have time to read the papers of the motion. Rehearsing out loud also gives the advocate a sense for whether he is wasting precious time in front of the judge regurgitating the same information written in the motion or reply.

5.7 Practice Discussing the Law Conversationally

The law should be discussed as conversationally as the facts that make up the storyline of the case. When discussing the law with the judge, pick the style that you would use to have a spirited debate with a friend at a restaurant. With that scenario in mind, you will be conversational and natural.

One of the unhappy byproducts of our legal education is the tendency to manipulate the language to make us "sound" like attorneys. Practice taking the legal talk out of your language. Avoid pretentious language that would sound awkward in a dinner conversation. That image alone should help you remove awkward transitional words such as "therefore," "hence," "moreover," and "notwithstanding." If for no other reason, take legal principles and transform them into conversational speech because *that* is a sign of true brilliance.

For those of you still reluctant to remove the legalese from your vernacular, consider the research of Danny Oppenheimer, Professor of Psychology at UCLA. In his paper entitled "Consequences of Erudite Vernacular Utilized Irrespective of Necessity: Problem with Using Long Words Needlessly,"[1] he concludes that audiences perceive overly complex language as a sign of low intelligence. A listener who must work hard to understand what an advocate is saying blames the advocate. If you feel like the judge failed to grasp the argument, the disconnect may be your own complicated language choices. Explain a legal theory in an organized, simple, and memorable way so that the message replays in the judge's mind. This can only happen with a conversational tone.

Exercise

Choose a legal theory within your motion or reply brief. Read the legal argument out loud as you record the delivery. Re-record the argument a second time describing the legal theory in a dramatically different and conversational tone—as if you were describing the theory to your best non-attorney friend. Limit this conversational delivery to two minutes. After you listen to yourself, ask, "How will the judge talk to a friend or spouse about the case? Her staff? Which version could she easily remember and replay in her head?"

If possible, call one colleague unfamiliar with your case. (A phone call will prevent non-verbal influences from changing your colleague's interpretation of the message.) Tell her you want her to listen to a legal argument and resist taking notes during your delivery. Read aloud the section of your papers that describes the legal theory you have chosen. Call a second colleague unfamiliar with the

---

1. See http://web.princeton.edu/sites/opplab/papers/opp%20consequences%20of%20erudite%20vernacular.pdf (last visited Aug. 19, 2016).

case. Ask him, too, to listen to a legal argument and resist taking notes during your delivery. Read your simple, conversational delivery—of no more than two minutes—to your second colleague. Wait a few hours and call both colleagues independently. Ask them how much they remember from the description delivered earlier in the day and write down their responses. Compare the difference in the remembered content.

5.8 Do Not Flip a Stylistic Switch

Some advocates have a dividing line in their minds between the facts and law. Often, an attorney is able to confidently and conversationally discuss the facts of the case, but the moment a legal argument begins, his voice or body language changes. There is a mental prejudice that the advocate has developed that makes him change the delivery style when he talks about the law. Perhaps he thinks he should categorically morph into a crotchety law professor and pontificate about the legal theories at issue. Perhaps he is less confident about the legal theories or is insecure about debating the law with a judge. Perhaps he thinks that anyone can deliver the facts, but only a bright attorney can discuss the law. The judge sees the change and it signals a problem. It raises a red flag of concern. Is the attorney hiding something? Is there a problem with the legal theory? Is there something I do not understand? Why is the attorney acting so differently?

Some notable changes include the pitfalls described in the table below.

IDENTIFYING THE PITFALL	EFFECT
Raising or lowering vocal pitch a note or two	Here, the speaker shifts the register of the voice entirely. Going up signals excitement, anxiety, questioning, or stress. Going down signals patronization, defeat, seriousness, or nonchalance.
Inserting upward inflection when introducing a new term to the court	This vocal pattern is a cousin of the upward inflection that causes a lift in the pitch of the voice at the ends of sentences. With upward inflection, or "upspeak," a speaker lifts the pitch of the voice irregularly running the risk of making him sound less intelligent and/or offending the judge by sounding patronizing. Either way, the advocate loses credibility and likability.
Accent changing	At times, attorneys with regional accents reduce the intensity of their natural accent when they switch to a more intellectual subject matter. The accent becomes neutralized. Assuming that the attorney's natural accent is inoffensive and comprehensible, there should be no shift in accent when he discusses law, facts, or public policy.

IDENTIFYING THE PITFALL	EFFECT
Noticeably crisper pronunciation	Like accent reduction, attorneys often over pronounce consonants when discussing the law as a way to force the listener to understand the theories.
Awkward vocal mistakes	Sometimes an attorney launches into a legal argument and clearly mispronounces names within the case. This breaks the rhythm of the speaker and makes the attorney look nervous or less prepared on the law. It would be better to take time on difficult words that are universally hard to pronounce and regain the previous pace of delivery.
Vacant facial expression	Sometimes an attorney forgets to match his facial expression with the themes and words of the law. The facial expression flattens and all expression is lost. There is not a better recipe for a boring delivery. Often, a judge loses interest in the legal argument section because the attorney removes all human connection or pathos with the information being delivered.
Marked change in posture	Some attorneys become so formal and rigid when discussing the law, they appear frozen and statuesque instead of confident.
Marked change in size, rate, or scope of gestures	All attorneys have natural gesticulation patterns. A telltale sign of nerves or discomfort with a position is a dramatic change from natural to over-controlled or exaggerated. Sometimes, attorneys use their natural gestures when discussing facts and look forced with a different gesticulation pattern when discussing the law.

Avoid the pitfall of changing the tone of your voice and/or your body language when talking about the law. Instead, stay consistent. Your discussion of law should be just as natural, comfortable, and seamless as the discussion of facts, greetings, and public policy.

Exercise

Audio-record yourself discussing the facts of a case and then discuss a legal theory of the case. If you detect a noticeable difference in your vocal delivery, then identify the change and practice saying the facts and law until the facts and law are discussed with the same vocal style.

Now video-record yourself discussing the facts of the case and then discuss a legal theory of the case. If you detect a noticeable difference in your body language, then identify the change and practice delivering the facts and the law until the same body language is used for both.

5.9   Do Not Read to the Judge

Judges, like most audiences, can read the brief and law more efficiently than having it read to them. When attorneys discuss the law, they often fall into the temptation of reading large sections of case law to the court. The motion hearing should be an oral discussion, not a reading. Here is the proper way to read a holding or a portion of case law to the court:

1)   Pick a powerful, on-point quote.

2)   Limit the reading to no more than two lines, but ideally one.

3)   Indicate to the court, with verbal and stylistic (body language and vocal) signaling, that you are quoting a statute, court, regulation, etc.

VERBAL SIGNALING
"As the court in *Hernandez* said . . ."
"As Judge Daniels determined . . ."
"As Chief Judge Roberts reasoned . . ."
"Congress clearly states . . ."
"The FTC gives us the standard of review . . ."

BODY LANGUAGE
Gesture to the front of your page as you begin to quote.
Show air quotes with your hands.
Change eye contact focus from the judge to the page.
Lift your eyes and re-connect with the judge immediately after or during the last moments of reading the quote.

VOCAL CHANGE
Raise or lower your pitch.
Slow down your delivery speed.
Pause.
Repeat a small portion (two to seven words) of the quote to launch into your next point with the court.

Chapter Six

Responding to Questions

Questions are your friends. Embrace them. Through questioning, you are able to glimpse into the judge's mind, his thinking process, and his struggles. And with this knowledge, you are able to respond in a way that addresses his individual and particular concerns. Nothing is more persuasive than to meet the judge precisely where he is—to respond to the very sticking points he has to decide the case in your favor. Questions from the judge should be welcomed—even cheered on—by you.

But, with questions come understandable anxiety. In the nerve-wracking tension of a hearing, many attorneys fear that not only will they not be able to answer a question, but they will also make a fool out of themselves. To be sure, there is an improvisational element to every hearing, but there are ways to plan for the unexpected. Of course, one of the best ways is to spend some time either alone or with others anticipating the questions you might be asked and your best responses to those inquiries.

No doubt, many queries can and will be anticipated before the hearing. However, in nearly every hearing, there will be times when the unexpected question is asked. This chapter gives you tools to deal with the spontaneity of the hearing. First, we will talk about a blueprint for answering questions. Then, we will talk about specific types of questions you are likely to be asked and how you can effectively answer them.

6.1 Steps to Answering Questions

Let's start with a six-step approach to answering questions. This formula should be used with every question asked.

STEPS TO ANSWERING A QUESTION

Step 1: Listen to the end of the question.

Step 2: Pause before you answer.

Step 3: Ask clarifying questions, if necessary.

Step 4: Directly answer the question first.

Step 5: Explain your answer.

Step 6: Transition back to your argument and your strengths.

6.1.1   Step One: Listen to the End of the Question

An attorney's tendency is to formulate the answer to a question before the question is complete. As the judge is asking questions, your mind may naturally drift to how you will concisely, intelligently, and persuasively answer the question. You may think that if you can create a proper response before the question is over, you will avoid the pregnant pause while you formulate your answer. Because multitasking is difficult for us all, you may stop listening to the question midstream to create the perfect comeback. Do not succumb to this tendency. Listen to the question until the end. Breathe. Take in the question.

To do otherwise means that mid-question, while you are contemplating your response, the question may take a twist—and by the time you are answering the question, it is not the question you have been asked. The evolving and sometimes changing question occurs because the hearing is spontaneous for the judge as well. As he is thinking about the case, questions arise on the spot as thoughts occur to him. And if he is creating his questions in the moment, then he will probably not be as succinct as he would be with planned questions. Questions twist and turn. To avoid answering the wrong question, listen until the judge is finished speaking. If you do not and the answer is a non-sequitur, you will lose your credibility—even if only slightly—with the judge, affecting your ability to persuade.

Further, even if you are firmly convinced that you know the question, do not answer the question before it is complete. Nothing is more rude and annoying to a judge than for an advocate to be so sure he knows where the question is going that to save time, he cuts off the judge before the judge has finished speaking. Impoliteness rarely makes you persuasive. *Never, never, never* talk over a judge.

6.1.2   Step Two: Pause Before You Answer

Pausing may be the most difficult part of this technique. Silence can be deafening and often seems longer than it really is. As a result, attorneys fill the space with chatter. Filler words like *um* and *so* are common. Also, attorneys say things like, "That was a good question, Judge." But, this inevitably leads the judge to say or think to himself, "Well, of course that was a good question, I asked it. Now answer it and stop wasting my time with false flattery."

Better to remain silent and take a deep breath to allow yourself a moment for your prefrontal cortex and its executive function to overtake the amygdala, the part of your brain associated with fear. Then categorize the question. What issue is implicated by the question? What type of question is it? Determine the judge's problem and where to go for its solution. Indeed, the judge is sincerely flattered that you are giving his question the thought that it is due. With his questions, the judge knows he is asking you to put together information in a way you have never thought about before.

Exercise

In everyday conversations, practice a pause pattern before answering questions. During the two-second silent pause, ask and answer to yourself two key questions: "What are they asking? Where do I go after I directly answer?"

Friend: "Did you like the movie?"

You, internally: Pause, and ask yourself, "What is he asking?" *I know him well. He is interested in the quality of the acting.* "Where do I go after I directly answer?" *I'll discuss Colin Firth's performance.*

You, aloud: "Yes. It's my favorite version of *Pride and Prejudice*. Colin Firth is the perfect Darcy . . . ."

6.1.3 Step Three: Ask Clarifying Questions, if Necessary

If you truly do not understand the question, ask for clarification. You may indicate to the judge that you do not know what he is asking you. Or you can begin to answer by indicating to the judge that you are taking his question to mean thus and so. The judge will then tell you whether you are right or wrong in your interpretation of the question.

There are important rules for clarifying a question:

- **Use this technique sparingly.** At the maximum, use it once during an argument.

- **Be interested and curious in your clarifying question, but do not apologize.** Many advocates apologize, which weakens their position. It sounds like this, "Judge, I am sorry, but I really do not understand the question you are asking." Chances are that it is not your fault that you do not understand the judge's question, so avoid saying you are sorry. During the course of your argument, there will be times you may need to apologize because you have misstated the facts, misconstrued a holding in a case, or otherwise misspoken. Save your apologies for the times you are truly wrong.

- **Do not use a clarifying question as a stalling technique.** If you understand the question, do not fill the silence of the pause while you think aloud with a clarifying question. Judges know when you are stalling. And if you ask a clarifying question more than once during the hearing, the judge will truly know you are delaying. Best to take a deep breath and relish in the silence while you construct your answer to a question you understand.

6.1.4   Step Four: Directly Answer the Question First

Many times you will be asked a direct question that requires a *yes* or *no* answer. Do not say that you will get to the answer later. The question is your first priority because it is the judge's priority. Answer "Yes," "No," or "It depends." If you do not, the judge will assume you are hedging. The judge's first impression will be that your position is weak; otherwise, you would confidently and straightforwardly answer the question. Evasion is also a catalyst for cross-examination. Remember, many judges are former trial attorneys. When a judge smells weakness, reflexively he tries out his rusty cross-examination skills—skills he was, or at least thinks he was, on top of at some point in his career.

Consider this scenario:

Judge: Does *Smith v. Smith* control the outcome in this case?

You: In *Smith v. Smith*, the husband had not paid child support for many years—

Judge: Counsel, is that a *yes*?

You: Well, it's not that simple. On the one hand, *Smith v Smith* is very similar to this case and on the other hand—

Judge: Then the short answer is *yes*?

You: I can't say that.

By the end of the colloquy, both the judge and you are frustrated. And the judge believes that you are vulnerable on the questioned point. Consider this conversation instead:

Judge: Does *Smith v. Smith* control the outcome in this case?

You: Yes, it does, Your Honor, and it supports our position because . . . .

Or:

You: No, it does not, Your Honor, and the reason it doesn't is . . . .

Give the short answer to a question that can be answered with a *yes, no,* or *it depends* before explaining your answer. Be careful to match your answer to your argument. The stronger your argument, the more definitive your answer can be. If you are weak in your answer—replying, for example, "It seems so"—yet your argument is strong, you have undermined your position. If, on the other hand, your answer is definitive, such as "It couldn't be clearer" and your argument is weak, you have diminished your credibility.

Here are some variations of the direct answer.

"YES"	"NO"	"IT DEPENDS"
"It seems so."	"No, that is not the case here."	"It's possible."
"Of course."	"Those aren't the facts."	"It's probable."
"You are correct."	"That's not possible."	"It's likely."
"There is no doubt."	"Certainly not."	"Maybe."
"It couldn't be clearer."	"Definitely not."	"Somewhat."
"Absolutely."	"Not at all."	"To some extent."
"Yes, and . . ."	"No, and . . ."	"It depends."

6.1.5   Step Five: Explain Your Answer

After you have answered the direct question, explain your answer. Rhetorically, decide how deeply you wish to cover the problem. Start where the judge is in his thinking process. Recognize the judge's concern inherent in the question. You will be more persuasive if, as you begin your argument, you show the court that you are on its side, even if briefly so. Consider the difference between the following scenarios:

> *Judge*: Explain to me why *Smith v. Jones* does not result in your client losing this motion.

> *You*: *Smith v. Jones* is totally distinguishable from this case.

Or:

> *You*: I understand your concerns with *Smith v. Jones*. In *Smith v. Jones*, the facts were *X, Y,* and *Z*, where here we have *X, Y,* and *B. B* makes the difference here because . . .

In the second scenario, you are more likely to persuade the court. In the first response, you are saying between the lines, "What's wrong with you, Judge? It is blatantly obvious that *Smith v. Jones* does not control at all—it's totally distinguishable." Much more persuasive was the second answer, when you acknowledged the judge's concern, validated it, and then gradually explained why the concern was unfounded. Begin your response by aligning yourself with the court, starting where the judge is. It allows the court to hear and be convinced by your argument. You can gradually return to your argument, the reassuring magic words of the law, and how the legal principles behind those magic words apply to your case.

Other rhetorical devices to persuade the court as to the appropriateness of your position are using the judge's or opposing counsel's words. Using the judge's words sides you with the court, making the distance you need to travel less to persuade him.

Suppose the opposing counsel in the above scenario is questioned about *Smith v. Jones*. You may answer, "As the court said before, *Smith v. Jones* does result in the other side losing the motion because . . . ." Again, you are aligning yourself with the court to highlight the correctness of the court's initial position. You can use the judge's words as an effective tool of persuasion. The same applies to opposing counsel's words. Great advocates turn the other side's words into their arguments, showing the vulnerability of the opposing argument.

Decide the Depth and Breadth of Your Answer

With each answer, you will need to decide how deeply and completely you want to delve into the problem. Through his questioning, a judge can hijack your argument. In the moment, decide when to expand, and when to contract, the answers. Is it better to give the short or long answer to the question? Your decision will be made on the spot and depends on the judge and the issue.

If you plunge too deeply into an issue, you risk losing the judge's interest—or worse yet, focusing on your weakness, a less persuasive strategy than focusing on your strength. However, if a judge has an interest in the issue, is struggling with it, or has an expertise in the area, a more extensive discussion is advisable.

The topic involved also informs the time you must spend on the answer. The more dependent your argument is on the point, the more time must be spent. Also, the weakness or strength of your argument factors into the coverage you give. If you are sure to win an argument, you may want to spend more time answering the question on those "iffier" arguments that you can win. On the other hand, if your point is particularly weak and not germane, then politely, concisely, and briefly respond to the point before quickly turning to your strengths. Overall, the amount of time you devote to a question depends on the judge's interest, concern, and struggle, along with the strength and centrality of the point to your argument.

Common Problems to Avoid

Two common problems occur during the questioning stage: biting back when the judge cuts you off and using weak language. As you know, cutting off the judge is taboo. Besides being impolite, it shows the judge you do not respect him. The judge may interrupt you—immediately stop speaking when you see the judge's lips move. And that means right in mid-sentence. You may be asking why you may not interrupt the judge but he may interrupt you. The answer is simple: he is the judge and decides your client's fate. In defense of judges, time is usually of the essence in a motion hearing and if the judge thinks your answer is going in a direction that is not productive to his resolution of the issue, he will stop you and veer you to a more productive avenue. Follow his lead.

Another common problem is weak or qualifying language. Answers that begin with "I think . . ." or "I believe . . ." undermine the strength of an argument.[1] The argument becomes interwoven with the personal credibility of the attorney. The attorney saying he believes the law is thus and so is not as strong as simply setting out the law. Instead of saying, "I think the law requires excusable neglect to set aside a default judgment," simply state, "The law says excusable neglect is required on the part of the defendant to set aside a default judgment." Examples of other credibility busters appear in the table below. These feeble phrases are usually wind-ups to avoid the discomfort of silence in a courtroom. Avoid the tendency to fill the silence by instead taking a breath and inserting a pause.

WHAT NOT TO SAY		
"I believe that . . ."	"I think . . ."	"I really feel like . . ."
"I really believe that . . ."	I'm not an expert but . . ."	"Just a thought."
"Take it for what it's worth."	If I could just say a few words about . . ."	"Just as long as we're throwing things out here, . . ."
"I'll get to that later."	"You know . . ."	"With all due respect . . ."
"I had sort of an idea about . . ."	"Go on, finish what you were saying."	"On the way to the court- house, . . ."

6.1.6   Step Six: Transition back to Your Argument and Your Strengths

Once you have explained your answer to the judge's question, transition back to your argument. The question is generally on a weakness in your position. Do not dwell on a weakness; rather, move back to your strengths. If you remain in defensive mode, defending your weaknesses, your argument will be weaker than offensively showcasing your strengths. Seguing to your main themes and subthemes will keep you on the offensive.

TRANSITIONAL LINES	
"And . . ."	"Because of that, . . ."
"This is exactly why . . ."	"That supports our position."
"Let's turn to . . ."	"With respect to . . ."
"This issue is similar to . . ."	"Let's unpack that."
"To summarize, . . ."	"Bottom line, . . ."
"This is symptomatic of a deeper issue."	"That brings us to the next point."
"That points to a hole in [insert party name]'s case."	"I share Your Honor's concern because . . ."

---

1. Current speaking trends of Millennials have an abnormally large number of qualifiers. Law school professors, partners, and supervisors should encourage young lawyers to shed qualifiers when answering questions to practice direct-answering techniques.

Think back to Planet Burger:

> *Judge*: Isn't a restaurant responsible for providing a minimum of safety to its patrons?

> *You*: Yes, Your Honor. And Planet Burger did provide more than the minimum. *This points to a hole in the plaintiffs' case*: they can't show that Planet Burger reasonably could have foreseen Kenneth Levy's reckless conduct.

As a review of the steps, for every question: listen to the question until it is finished, pause, ask clarifying questions if necessary, answer the direct question first, explain your answer, and then transition back to your strengths. Before we turn to types of questions and what to do to answer each kind, let's set up a hypothetical case involving a well-known fairy tale and use it to provide concrete responses to the various forms of questions.

6.2 *Humpty Dumpty v. The King*

A default judgment was entered against the King in the civil complaint that Humpty Dumpty filed against him for negligence.[2] Counsel represents the King in a hearing to set aside the default judgment. Prior counsel had his head cut off.

The facts are that Humpty Dumpty climbed the wall surrounding the King's castle. He was able to climb to the top because embedded in the wall were pieces of rebar that formed a makeshift ladder. From his vantage point, Mr. Dumpty was able to peer inside the King's chambers. In any event, we all know what happened from there, after which Mr. Dumpty filed his negligence lawsuit against the King.

Mr. Dumpty served the King's men, who promptly took the complaint and summons to the Imperial Law Firm—the firm who routinely handled the King's legal matters. The firm's administrative assistants gave the paperwork to the senior partner, the Emperor, who had been the King's personal attorney for years. Unfortunately, the Emperor had a mental breakdown, ran through the kingdom naked, and proclaimed he had new clothes. The Emperor's family committed him after the incident. The complaint was not answered. Mr. Dumpty's attorney moved for a default judgment against the King, which the court granted. Two months later, counsel moved to set aside the default judgment.

The pertinent legal authority in the kingdom is Trial Rule (TR) 60(b), *Everystate v. Big Bad Wolf,* and *Old Witch v. Hansel and Gretel.* TR 60(b) allows a court to set aside a default judgment *only* upon a showing of excusable neglect *and* a meritorious defense. The concept of excusable neglect was examined by the court of appeals

---

2. Judge Nancy Vaidik originally created this fact scenario as a teaching tool used in conjunction with the National Institute of Trial Advocacy's custom Motion Practice course. Through the years, talented attorneys, such as Michael Dale, an extraordinarily gifted professor at Nova Southeastern Law School whose life mission has been to advocate for children, have added a few fun details to the story.

in *Everystate v. Big Bad Wolf.* There, the insurance company, Everystate, filed a declaratory judgment action against its insured, the Big Bad Wolf, claiming that it was not liable for the intentional acts of the Big Bad Wolf in blowing down the houses of the three pigs. The declaratory judgment was granted by default because Wolf's counsel, Jack and Jill LLP, did not answer Everystate's complaint. Jack and Jill claimed that they were unable to do so because of injuries they themselves had sustained near the time of service of the complaint. The appellate court affirmed the trial court's decision to set aside the default judgment against Wolf. In *Old Witch v. Hansel and Gretel*, the appellate court sustained a jury's finding that the Old Witch had created an attractive nuisance, luring Hansel and Gretel into her house. Neither case discussed prejudice, the burden of showing prejudice, or the potential malpractice claim against the defaulting law firm.

For purposes of illustrating the various types of questions likely to be asked at a motion hearing, assume that counsel argues for the default judgment to be set aside.

6.3 Types of Questions

There is a universe of possible questions a judge can ask at a motion hearing. We characterize those questions, name them, and give suggestions as to how to respond to each.

6.3.1 *The Kickoff Question*

Often, a judge kicks off the motion with confrontational questions. An attorney must be ready to jump cleanly into a legal argument without confusing the judge and simultaneously prove the need for the judge to hear the argument.

- "Counselor, what can you tell me today that isn't already in your papers?"

  "I can tell you facts that have developed since we wrote the papers."

- "Why are we having this motion? Can't I make a ruling off your written motion?"

  "We stand by our written motion, but I'm here to discuss the motion with you, Your Honor."

- "Why do you want to argue this today?"

  "I wanted a chance to discuss your concerns that were raised on our last phone conference. Those concerns are valid, and they are in line with our request today."

- "Why did you need an hour of the court's time?"

  "Your decision today will help both parties settle this matter, and we wanted sufficient time to discuss the issues with you."

- "You aren't here to tell me things you failed to argue in your papers, are you?"

"No, Your Honor. I'm here to highlight issues and answer your concerns."

THE KICKOFF	
General	The initial question asked by a court. Be ready to jump in right away.
Words	"Your Honor, I'm here to highlight issues and answer your concerns." "I can tell you facts that have developed since we wrote the papers." "Let me bring you up to speed since the last time we spoke, Your Honor."
Voice	Clear, projected
Body Lan-guage	Athletic home base, calm gestures
Tone	Warm and engaging

6.3.2   The "I Don't Know" Question

One of the most terrifying types of questions is the one to which you do not know the answer. Of course, the best way to avoid this question is to anticipate it before the hearing. But sometimes, even most times, no matter the preparation, you are not able to predict every question. If you do not know the answer, in most instances the best course is to admit that you do not know, offer a process to find the solution, and engage the judge in order to find and discuss the problem.

Judges have a good ear as to when counsel is dodging a question. And the more that is said, the easier it is to spot the fudge. There are many ways to say "I don't know."

WAYS TO SAY "I DON'T KNOW"
"I'm not sure, but I do know . . . ."
"I'm not familiar with that . . . ."
"I was not aware of that."
"That doesn't seem to be what we have here . . . ."
"I'm unclear on the details."
"That's not in the record . . . ."
"I'm not certain and don't want to tell you anything that is inaccurate."
"I don't have that at my fingertips. If you give me a moment, my colleague can provide that cite."
"That case does not appear in any of the papers filed."

After saying that you do not know, offer a solution. If the question pertains to a particular case, then you may feel confident enough in the area of law to ask the court to briefly provide you with details of the case to trigger your memory. If you recall, then you will have avoided calamity. If not, then candidly admit that nothing was sparked in your memory. In any event, offer a solution, such as submitting supplemental briefing on the issue within twenty-four hours. After offering to provide supplemental papers, try to engage the court in a discussion to determine the nature of the problem. You may be able to clear up the difficulty without the need to file additional papers.

Example

Humpty Dumpty v. The King

Judge: How about the *Little Red Riding Hood* case?

Counsel: I am not familiar with the case, Your Honor. I would be happy to brief it and provide supplemental papers in twenty-four hours. Is the court concerned with the assumption of risk?

Do not wither when responding to a question for which you do not know the answer. Avoid looking shocked or surprised. Show interest in the judge's question. Stand upright, no slumped shoulders. In a clear understandable voice, respond that you do not know the answer but will get back to the court. While answering, be careful not to lift your inflection as if you are asking the court a question.

You may answer that you do not know only once or twice in a long hearing before you lose your credibility. Your best defense against the question you cannot answer is always preparation.

Exercise

Practice in front of a mirror the "I don't know" response.

- Is your posture confident?

- Are you slumping your shoulders?

- Have you practiced the words enough so you do not stumble over them?

- Are you maintaining the volume of your voice?

- Are you avoiding the upward inflection of your voice so you do not sound like you are asking a question?

- Do you look and sound confident?

Practice this exercise until your responses are automatic and you look comfortable with saying you do not know.

6.3.3 The "Outside the Record" Question

Sometimes the judge asks a question where the answer requires a response with information that is not in the record. If you do not know the answer, then tell the court you are unable to answer. However, if you know the answer but the answer is not found in the record submitted to the court, tell the judge that the information is not part of the record. Then ask him if you should answer the question. If he says you should, then do so.

Example

Humpty Dumpty v. The King

Judge: Is the Holy Grail located in such a position in the King's chambers that someone who scaled the wall could see it?

Counsel: The answer to the question is not in the court's record. Would you like me to answer it anyway?

Judge: Yes.

Counsel: No, the Holy Grail is locked and hidden in a safe.

6.3.4 The Softball Question

The softball is the easy question—the one you cannot wait to answer. With a multi-judge panel, the judge favorable to your position may be speaking to another judge on the bench through his questions to you.

The first step is to recognize the softball. It may be delivered in an angry tone so the judge does not show his cards to the opposing counsel. The angry tone may throw you off as well. Do not let it. Instead, take advantage of the softball and hit it out of the park. Take the opportunity to give your sixty-second elevator speech on the issue.

An example of a common softball question in a summary judgment hearing is: "What are the material facts at issue here?" Or in a discovery hearing: "Tell me how this request is relevant to your case?" or "I see no alternative but to . . . ." If the judge does tip his hand in the question, lean into the answer and take the opportunity to side with the judge.

THE SOFTBALL QUESTION
"Absolutely, Your Honor."
"That's precisely why it matters."
"Yes, Your Honor."
"I absolutely agree."
"Yes, that's correct."
"Yes, we see this the same way."

As soon as you recognize the softball, you may nod your head in agreement with the judge, but not obnoxiously so. Try taking a step back from counsel table in order to give the judge the floor. Answer in a warm and pleasant manner. Deliver your points that align with the court in a slower-paced rhythm. Do not become arrogant, or the judge may change his mind. No one likes a know-it-all. Be gracious in your win.

Example

Humpty Dumpty v. The King

Judge: Doesn't *Everystate v. Big Bad Wolf* completely resolve this case?

Counsel: Yes, it absolutely does, Your Honor. *Everystate* stands for the fundamental proposition that everyone deserves his day in court. Even the Big Bad Wolf. Just as the King deserves his day in court.

6.3.5   *The Genuine Inquiry*

The genuine inquiry is a little different from the softball question. Unlike the softball, with the genuine inquiry the judge is not leaning toward your position. The judge is sincerely asking you to teach him the law and/or the facts. Basically, he is admitting that he does not know, but wants you to explain it to him.

Your response should be helpful. Take the opportunity to go deeper into the issue. Do not respond with the obsequious, "That is a good question, Your Honor." Neither should you point out the deficiency of the judge's knowledge with, "Many misunderstand that holding." Nor should you tell the judge that "it is complicated," implying that it is too difficult for him to understand. Be patient, not belittling. Instead, use the opportunity for a moment to clarify and explain. Assume the senior law clerk position. Do not lecture. Keep an even volume, measured-paced voice, with the range narrowed. Speak as if you were talking to your parents across the kitchen table. And most of all, be excited because the questions do not get better than this. This is your opportunity to connect with the judge, and to convince him of your point of view.

Genuine inquiry questions give you a further chance to connect with the judge by using his very words in your answer. By doing so, you let the judge know that you are listening to and understanding his struggle—and you are there to help.

If you notice a judge continually asking about an issue or fact, do not ignore it. Do not interpret that questioning as an assault. The judge is telling you that he needs help with that issue. Help him.

THE GENUINE INQUIRY
"I'd be happy to, Your Honor."
"That brings us deeper into the issue of . . . ."
"I would be glad to elaborate."
Note: You can also use the judge's words to begin your answer.

Example

Humpty Dumpty v. The King

Judge: Was the Emperor ill?

Counsel: He was ill. Extremely ill. So ill that he was wandering the streets of the kingdom naked. The King apparently did all he could to answer the complaint by giving it to the Emperor, and, but for the illness of the Emperor, it would have been answered. This is classic excusable neglect, and neither side would be prejudiced by setting aside the default.

6.3.6   *The Hostile Question and the Insistent Judge*

You will know immediately from the tone and content of a judge's question that the judge is not buying what you are selling. Often, the question starts with something like, "You are not saying . . . ?" And that is exactly what you are saying. Find the ground between shrinking and wrestling. Begin by politely holding your position. Try to reason with the court. Test the waters. As you stand your ground, do not appear aggressive. Lower the pitch of your voice and slow your pace. Now is *not* the time to take a fighter's stance in the courtroom. Instead, place your palms upward and take a step back, so as not to appear aggressive. Make sure your facial expressions reflect concern, and not annoyance.

If the judge persists in the hostile questioning, do not wrestle—disengage. When it becomes clear that you will not convince the judge on a particular point, it is time to change directions. Either pull out one of the other independent arguments you prepared, or turn the court's attention to another aspect of this issue. This is where preparing alternative arguments pays off. You need to let the court know that there is nothing more you can say on the contentious point and you would like to move on. Agree to disagree. Otherwise, all your time can be chewed up arguing this losing point.

Do not misinterpret formality for hostility. Some advocates recoil when questions are asked from a formal judge. Because the attorney mistakes the judge's formality for impatience, she foregoes a chance to connect with the judge. If the formal judge asks you a question, answer it.

HOSTILE QUESTIONS FROM AN INSISTENT JUDGE
"There is nothing more I can add to this discussion. May I move on?"
"Sadly, we must agree to disagree on this point, but we still win because . . . ."
"I'm disappointed we don't agree on this point, Judge. May I move to my next point?"
"It sounds to me like we will have to agree to disagree, but I'm hoping you'll agree with me on . . . ."
"May I explain why I disagree?"

The most important lesson here is, do not let the court shake you. Keep calm. Stay true to your integrity and personality.

Example

Humpty Dumpty v. The King

Judge: This case is completely resolved by *Old Witch v. Hansel and Gretel*. The King created an attractive nuisance here, just as the Old Witch did. The King has no meritorious defense. Tell me why this isn't so?

Counsel: The facts of this case are very dissimilar to *Old Witch*. In *Old Witch*—

Judge: I just can't agree with you, counsel. In *Old Witch*, candy was dripping from the cottage, and here, Mr. Dumpty could see into the King's chambers.

Counsel: True, but like *Old Witch*, the jury should decide whether there is an attractive nuisance.

Judge: I disagree with you, counsel.

Counsel: It seems we have a different understanding of *Old Witch*. If I could turn the court's attention to another example of attractive nuisance with *Jack and the Beanstalk* . . . .

6.3.7 *The Hypothetical Question*

A hypothetical question is a "what if" question. What if the facts of the case were tweaked in one respect or another, would the result be the same? Hypothetical questions are common for two reasons. One, because the "what if" scenario may come before the court in the future and the court wants to be consistent. Or two, the judge enjoys the intellectual banter because it reminds him of the Socratic discussions of law school. In either case, the hypothetical question is difficult to prepare for, as it is difficult to anticipate every future factual situation.

Your inclination is to immediately point out that the hypothetical question does not reflect the facts of your case. Resist the temptation. Of course the facts are different. Preparing clean analogies to your facts will help differentiate the judge's hypothetical with a more perfect analogy.

Because hypotheticals can be confusing, you may need to begin your answer by confirming and clarifying the details. Fully engage with the judge so you may identify what is driving the judge in asking the question. Say to the judge, "If I understand your hypothetical correctly, the situation you describe involves . . . ."

After you fully understand the specific question, answer with "Yes, the result would be the same," "No, it wouldn't," "It depends," or "I am not sure." If you do not, the judge will think that you are hedging because of the weakness of your argument.

Understandably, many attorneys who appear before the same court on the same type of cases, such as prosecutors or other government attorneys, are reticent to answer definitively one way or another for fear they will be bound to their answer if the theoretical comes true in a future case. In that event, the attorney must balance the likelihood of the hypothetical occurring against the impact the equivocation might have on the result of the case at hand. An "it depends" or "I am not sure" answer, with an explanation, may be the best course for this concern.

After answering the direct question, explain your answer. During the explanation, distinguish the facts of the hypothetical from the facts of your case. Let the court know that in his ruling he does not need to go as far as the hypothetical takes him.

THE HYPOTHETICAL QUESTION
"As I understand it . . . ."
"In your hypothetical, the facts are . . . ."
"Yes, under those circumstances, the court would dismiss the matter . . . ."
"It depends . . . ."
"No, Your Honor. That would not change the decision."
"It may, but one major difference with the scenario is . . . ."
"Your Honor, the court doesn't need to go that far. All we are asking for is . . . ."

When answering the hypothetical, have a sporting attitude instead of one of dread. Your tone and facial expressions should be welcoming. Enjoy the intellectual exercise. If you have pre-planned analogies to compare with the court's, the hypothetical question can be an amazing intellectual exchange with the judge.

Example

Humpty Dumpty v. The King

Judge: Would it have made any difference if a carnival was inside the King's wall at the time Mr. Dumpty scaled the wall?

Counsel: Yes, if there were a carnival inside the King's wall, then it would be more likely an attractive nuisance. With a carnival, there would be rides, music, children's laughter, and the smell of popcorn. But, here there was none of that excitement. Here, there was rebar and stone walls. Even so, whether an attractive nuisance exists is a question for a trier of fact. The King deserves his day in court.

Or:

Counsel: No. Of course a carnival inside the walls would be more enticing—the smell of popcorn, children's laughter, rollercoasters, music—but even so, the trier of fact would decide whether the King created an attractive nuisance. The facts here are more like a Peeping Tom peering into Sleeping Beauty's dressing room. The King deserves his privacy, and, like anyone else, should be afforded the opportunity to have a jury decide this issue.

6.3.8   The Rabbit Hole

When a judge asks questions that stray you off your themes and often times into the weeds of opposing counsel's counterarguments, it is necessary to back out of the rabbit hole and bring the court back to your main themes. Listen to the court's concerns, but do not feel compelled to follow the judge down an intellectual path that is ultimately irrelevant to the motion at hand. Affirm the concern and shift back to a major theme.

Be bold in leading the judge in the right direction. Do not be brash. Increase the volume of your voice to show you know what you are talking about.

THE RABBIT HOLE QUESTION
[*answer quickly and directly*] " . . . . but today we are here for the court to decide . . . ."
"I share your concern with fairness, and right now, the issue that faces us *is* ultimately about fairness."
"That discussion sends us on a detour, which I'm happy to discuss."

> **Example**
>
> ***Humpty Dumpty v. The King***
>
> *Judge*: Talk to me about how sovereign immunity affects the King's case.
>
> *Counsel*: Mr. Dumpty may raise that at a future time, but right now the issue is whether the King has had his day in court.

6.3.9   The Confused Judge

The confused judge is just that: confused. He may be confused about what case is before him. He may be puzzled about the history of the case. He may not understand the nature of the proceedings before him.

In defense of the befuddled judge, motions days can be hectic. Patiently bring the confused judge back to your case.

Avoid the look of shock, surprise, or disgust. Lead the judge back with a relaxed posture, expanded gestures to help explain the substance, and a slowed pace of voice.

THE CONFUSED JUDGE
"Your Honor, today's motion focuses on . . . ."
"I understand your concern, but today we're here to . . . ."
"The point is . . . ."
"This case concerns . . . ."

> **Example**
>
> ***Humpty Dumpty v. The King***
>
> *Judge*: Didn't I already set aside the default judgment?
>
> *Counsel*: No, Your Honor. Today, we are here asking you to do just that for the following reasons . . . .

6.3.10   The Misinformed Judge

The misinformed judge is a subset of the confused judge. This judge mistakes the facts or the law. You are ethically bound to correct him even if his misunderstanding favors your position. In the long run, your credibility will be enhanced. But, be diplomatic. Do not say: "No, you are wrong, Your Honor." Instead: "Counsel for the other side is right about *X*, but we win anyway because . . . ." If appropriate, take the blame for the misunderstanding. Return to your theme to help refocus the judge's attention.

THE MISINFORMED JUDGE
"Counsel is correct in this, but we win anyway because . . . ."
"The holding in *X* was not . . . . but it does not make a difference because . . . ."
"Just to set the record straight, the facts here are . . . ."
"Perhaps I have not been clear."

Example

Humpty Dumpty v. The King

Judge: Counselor, since Humpty Dumpty leapt off the wall, doesn't that necessarily mean that the King wins?

Counsel: To be clear, Mr. Dumpty fell off the wall, but the King still wins because Mr. Dumpty was a trespasser.

6.3.11 The Suspicious Judge

There is a natural, learned suspicion in judges. They will rarely be open and friendly from the start. You must earn it. Do not take it personally; rather, use the opportunity to win the judge's trust. Return any coldness or distance with warmth and professionalism.

Sometimes, you know ahead of time, or through the course of the motion, that the judge does not like or trust you or your client. Recognize that his distrust may not be personal against you. He may distrust the client, your co-counsel, or a previous counsel on the matter.

When answering the suspicious judge's questions, maintain longer than usual eye contact to show your sincerity. Slow down the pace of your voice. Do not mirror the tone of the question. Stay calm and professional. Keep your palms up when gesturing to underscore your openness. Be careful not to exaggerate or overstate. Use exhibits to corroborate the veracity of your statements.

Example

Humpty Dumpty v. The King

Judge: You didn't file your request to set aside the default judgment until two months after the judgment was entered?

Counsel: Yes, we did, Your Honor. If you would take a look at the file stamp on the judgment and then look at the file stamp on the motion to set it aside, you will see it was actually a little less than two months. I have copies of those two documents, if you would like me to approach.

6.3.12   The "Let's Make a Deal" Discussion

During a motion hearing, opportunities arise to negotiate a resolution of the motion or the case with the court or opposing counsel through the court. Recognize that underneath the chatter, bargaining is occurring. Use the occasion to find win-win solutions.

"Why haven't you settled?" may be the most asked question by any trial court judge at a motion hearing. Be prepared with an answer. Do not disparage your opponent by responding that this should have settled but for the unreasonableness of the other side. Doing so will provoke a counterattack muddying both of you. Instead, let the court know that both parties have tried to settle the case, but are not there yet. Then use the inquiry to show the court that resolution of this motion, in your favor, will go a long way to ending the case.

When asked the question, show the court that you would also like to settle the case by nodding your head in agreement. You may be thinking that the court is trying to avoid its responsibility to decide the case, but do not show your annoyance. Keep a poker face.

"WHY HAVEN'T YOU SETTLED?" RESPONSES
"We have tried to find a solution and may still, but we are not there yet."
"We share your desire for resolution, and your decision on this motion will help to settle this case [or, if the motion is dispositive, will end the case]."
"A ruling will help move the parties in the right direction. Let me show you how."
"We need your guidance, Your Honor, and a ruling on this motion will give us the direction we need."

Sometimes the court initiates negotiations by expressing its concerns and offering proposed solutions. Seldom does the court outright tell you that it will rule one way if you concede a point. Often, you must read between the lines. Consider this exchange:

Example

Humpty Dumpty v. The King

Judge: I may be inclined to set aside the default judgment, but this may be a long, arduous, and costly process for the King . . . .

Counsel: I understand your concern, Your Honor. [*Pause.*] Would an offer of $100,000 settle this matter today?

Notice that the court did not expressly indicate it was negotiating, but counsel got the message and made a judgment call. The judgment call was not likely made on the spot. Before the hearing, counsel anticipated this discussion and had a number prearranged and preapproved by the client.

Sometimes the court does not offer a solution; rather, you or opposing counsel propose solutions based on the court's concerns. These discussions are often the turning point of a hearing. Even if the conversations do not resolve the case or motion at the moment, try to discern what matters most to the opposing party and its counsel. This information will help facilitate and inform future settlement negotiations.

During these bargaining sessions, show the court that you are a partner with it in trying to find a solution. If you not able to accept the solutions offered, explain why you cannot.

"LET'S MAKE A DEAL" RESPONSES (WHEN YOU CAN'T ACCEPT THE PROPOSAL)
"I can't go as far as you want, but I can . . . ."
"I am having trouble with this one small aspect of your request . . . ."
"I need to consult with my client to get approval."
"I regret that we are too far down the road to accept this proposal."

> **Example**
>
> ***Humpty Dumpty v. The King***
>
> *Judge*: Counselor, by setting aside this default judgment, I will be prolonging the case to the detriment of the plaintiff. Isn't that true?
>
> *Counsel*: We are willing to fast-track this case to avoid that problem.

6.3.13 Concessions

Often a judge will ask you to concede certain points. The judge may want to clarify the nature of your request or limit the issues he must decide. Or it may be that the judge wants to decrease his risk of being reversed on appeal. In any case, concessions can be dangerous territory.

First decide if you are able to concede. Think through the logical long-term and short-term consequences of conceding. The judge may be asking for a concession that will produce a domino effect, lulling you into a cascade of concessions.

You should concede when it does not hurt your client and only if your client approves. Show you are elated to be able to make this allowance. If you refuse to concede when there is no down side of doing so, you will be perceived as unreasonable—the gladiator attorney who fights for the fight alone. Once you take such a stance, prepare to engage in combat with the judge. The judge will repeatedly and incredulously ask you why you refuse to concede, thereby wasting valuable time, angering the judge, and hurting your credibility.

On the other hand, if you cannot concede because it will hurt your client's case to do so, *hold your ground*. Be firm. Depending on the circumstances, be disappointed that you are unable to concede. But do not blame the lack of a concession on your client. If you need time to prepare a response, it is all right to say that you need time to talk to your client, but if after you have talked and you are still unable to concede, do not blame it on your client. Explain to the court the reason, in fairness, you are unable to concede.

If you find yourself in a situation where you believe it may hurt the case to concede but the upside outweighs the downside, you must talk to your client before you can yield. To not do so may cause you ethical issues.

WHEN YOU CAN CONCEDE
"Yes, Your Honor, my client can agree to that."
"We are happy to stipulate to that, but we ask the court to . . . ."
"I agree, Your Honor, that is correct, but it doesn't affect the ultimate result because . . . ."

WHEN YOU CANNOT CONCEDE
"I have to talk to my client before we can agree to that."
"Your Honor, that's not going to work in this situation."
"We can't waive that, Your Honor."
"There are far greater consequences that prevent me from agreeing."
"We cannot concede that, and the reason is . . . ."

> **Example**
>
> ***Humpty Dumpty v. The King***
>
> *Judge*: Aren't there other attorneys in the Emperor's firm who could have handled this case?
>
> *Counsel*: Yes, there are, Your Honor, but no one had the relationship with the King that the Emperor had. And that's because the Emperor had personally represented the King for twenty-three years . . . .
>
> Or:
>
> *Counsel*: No, only the Emperor had the knowledge, background, and relationship with the client to handle this case. And, it was excusable for the King to rely on the Emperor . . . .

6.3.14 *Engaging the Disengaged Judge*

What do you do when the judge does not engage with you at all? Perhaps he makes no eye contact; perhaps he says nothing; perhaps he is checking his phone; perhaps is he obviously flipping through your brief for the first time. You have no clue whatsoever what he is thinking about your motion. This is the time when your long script comes in handy.[3] Before you resort to only giving your long script, however, try to find ways to capture the judge's attention.

Change the pace or volume of your speech. Increase the speed to show passion or excitement—or noticeably slow down your speech. Increase the volume of your voice—or decrease the volume to a whisper to make an important point. Maybe the change—fast or slow pace, low or high volume—will attract the judge's interest.

---

3. We cover long and short scripting techniques in Chapter Seven.

Silence can also act as an attention grabber. Use a long, three-second pause while you search through your notes, for an extra moment of silence in hopes of alerting the judge. Or try clearing your throat.

Use an exhibit. Have an extra copy of a pertinent case, ask to approach the bench to hand the case to the judge, and point out a passage particularly relevant from the case. Highlight and cite to a deposition excerpt. During a hearing on a 12(b)(6) motion to dismiss, refer the court to a portion of the complaint to highlight that there are no facts upon which relief can be granted. Or use a slideshow or a poster that you have prepared ahead of time. Utilizing a demonstrative or visual aid, at worst, requires some court participation and, at best, may spur a discussion.

If these strategies do not work, the court is likely just going through the motions—pun intended—of a hearing. Revert to your long script that you prepared before the hearing. The monologue should be no longer than five minutes for a short motion and no longer than ten minutes for a longer hearing. You will not hold the court's attention for any longer, and your long script reflects your best-crafted and most concise arguments. The court will also appreciate your brevity.

Example

Humpty Dumpty v. The King

Counsel: If I could draw your attention to page 15, lines 14 to 18 of the deposition of the managing partner of the Imperial Law Firm. [*Silence to allow the court time to find the citation. Once the judge has indicated he has found the citation and read the passage, counsel continues.*] This is the testimony indicating the condition of the Emperor at the time the King was served the complaint. You will see that the Emperor . . . .

6.3.15   *The Guillotine*

Unfortunately, there comes a time when you know that you have lost. Cheerfully exit. Avoid pouting or lashing out at the judge. Do not threaten the judge with an appeal. Judges, like anyone else, do not cower upon threat. If anything, your attempt at intimidation may make the judge work harder to reverse-proof his order. Neither should you thank a judge when you have been defeated.

Instead, exit gracefully. Be polite and professional. This will not be the last time you are before the judge. If you need to make a record for appeal, do so, but do not whine and repeat what you have already said.

Usually, you should not ask the court to reconsider its decision during the hearing. The prospects of the judge changing his mind on the spot are limited. If you do have new arguments that you think may sway the judge, then ask for reconsideration based on the other reasons. Otherwise, if you think the court may change its mind after reflection, file papers asking for reconsideration.

RESPONSES TO THE GUILLOTINE COMMENT/QUESTION
"I would like to make the record clear that . . . ."
"Your Honor, I do need to make a record that . . . ."
"I understand the Court's position, although obviously I disagree for the reasons I have stated."
"I would ask the court to reconsider because [*new reasons*]."
"I do have one more argument I would ask the court to consider."

Example

Humpty Dumpty v. The King

Judge: Counsel, I see no reason to set aside this default judgment. Judicial economy supports my decision.

Counsel: I understand your concern. I do have a point that we have not discussed, namely, judicial economy may not be served by upholding this judgment. If the judgment remains, the King will have a malpractice claim against the Imperial Law Firm. So one way or another, the court will have to resolve the merits of this claim. The King deserves his day in court.

6.3.16   The Win

There may come a time when you know you have won. Stop talking immediately. When opposing counsel has dug herself into a very deep hole and the judge says, "There is nothing more you can add, is there, counsel?" Politely say no and sit down. Do not snatch defeat from the jaws of victory.

6.4   Multi-Judge Panels

All of these suggestions also apply to multi-judge panels. You may find yourself before an appellate court, multiple judges in multidistrict litigation, or a judge and his magistrate. With more than one judge, there are additional considerations.

6.4.1   Who Is in Charge Here?

To the extent you are able, find out whose opinion counts for more on the panel. Sometimes, no judge dominates the decision making—sometimes, one does. If you are confident that one judge's opinion is given more weight in the panel, then tailor your argument to that judge. Be careful though. If you are wrong, you run the risk of perturbing the other judges. Even if you think one judge is dominant, do not give that judge more eye contact. Judges notice if they are being ignored. Do not risk alienating anyone.

6.4.2   Eye Contact

Listen with your eyes when a judge asks you a question, maintaining complete eye contact with that judge during his question. When you answer the question, spend the first fifteen seconds focused on the judge who asked the question. Then open up your eye contact and body language to include all the judges. Make sure you switch eye contact after completing a thought with each judge (three to four seconds each). Return to the original judge to conclude your answer, locking eyes again and watching for non-verbal clues that confirm you answered the question.

6.4.3   The "I Don't Know" Question

Pause an additional second or two if you do not know the answer. This allows time for a judge favorable to your position to rescue you if he is so inclined. If there is no lifeboat floated your way, there is no downside to the pause.

6.4.4   The Softball Question

Continue eye contact with the judge who asks the softball until the question is finished. Recognize, though, that the asking judge wants you to convince his colleagues. So spend the majority of your answer time connecting with the non-questioning judges.

6.4.5   The Hostile Question from a Hijacking Judge

This judge wants to convince his colleagues through his question to you. This judge will continue to insist, and there is nothing else you can say. You are really talking to the other judges. If the judge continues to interrupt and insist, then agree to disagree and move on. Try not to get offended when a judge turns hostile, especially in front of the other observing judges. They often see the abusive judge as the aggressor if you resist the urge to fight back. If you engage and fight the judge, the listening judges will eventually decide against you and protect their colleague.

6.4.6   The Crossfire Question

Often, the judges are asking questions, but they are talking to one another. They are in a debate. Sometimes your best technique is to watch and listen, unless the debate sways against you. Without interrupting any judge, insert clarification or reorient the discussion if the debate starts turning against your position.

6.4.7   The "Let's Make a Deal" Discussion

Be careful negotiating with one judge on the panel. If the judge is not the decision maker, you may be giving up something you may not have to because the majority of the panel is with you. When it becomes clear, though, that all judges are drawn to the deal and you and your client can live with it, then negotiate away. Still, concede those points that do not hurt you, regardless of whether all judges are on board.

6.5   Oh, Yeah, and . . .

Provide the judge with your undivided attention. It goes without saying, but give the judge your undivided attention. No "multi-tasking" or "rapid refocus."

Your motion time should be spent discussing the issues with the judge, not your co-counsel. Do not chat with co-counsel during the motion. If the judge asks you for a citation, page number, or case name you do not have handy, ask the judge if he wants you or your co-counsel to find the paper or jump cite. If the judge asks a question to which your co-counsel knows the answer better than you, respond accordingly: "Your Honor, my colleague Ms. White can give you more detail about the technology behind this section of the patent." If the judge directly asks your co-counsel a question, let her answer it.

Also, do not speak directly to opposing counsel during the motion. Make your arguments to the judge, not to the opposing attorney.

Do not minimize or trivialize the judge's question or confusion. When you take this approach, you miss out on a huge opportunity. Instead of using belittling transition lines—"Your Honor, the real issue is . . ."—rejoice. The right approach is to affirm and address the issue—and be thrilled to discover the concern of the court. That is why you are there.

Observe the emotions behind the words. Notice if the judge is cheerful, interested, angry, afraid, frustrated, or resentful. Respond to the emotion as well as the words. Observe all verbal and nonverbal cues, including tone, facial expressions, and other body language. It takes repetition and exposure to read any particular judge.

Enjoy the repartee of the questions. You will find that the questions make your presentation more convincing. While initially you may think that the discussion is difficult, soon you will see that the monologue is more difficult because you have no idea whether your words are making any impact. But with questioning, you meet the judge precisely where he is in his thinking, make those arguments that are most convincing to him, and are seen as a problem-solving partner.

	THE KICKOFF	GUILLOTINE	ENGAGING THE DISENGAGED JUDGE
General	The initial question asked by a court. Be ready to jump in right away.	Exit gracefully. Be polite and professional. This will not be the last time you are before the judge. If you need to make a record for appeal, do so, but do not whine and repeat what you have already said. If you do have new arguments that you think may sway the judge, then ask for reconsideration based on the other reasons.	The goal is to get judge's attention politely and professionally.
Words	"Your Honor, I'm here to highlight issues and answer your concerns." "I can tell you facts that have developed since we wrote the papers." "Let me bring you up to speed since the last time we spoke, Your Honor."	"I would like to make the record clear that . . . ." "Your Honor, I do need to make a record that . . . ." "I understand the Court's position, although obviously I disagree for the reasons I have stated." "I would ask the court to reconsider because [*new reasons*]."	If all attempts fail, use your long script.
Voice	Clear, projected.	Calm and slow. Stay away from high pitches.	Increase volume. Big change in pace. Long pause.
Body	Athletic home base, calm gestures.	Relax shoulders and avoid lunging on the podium. If necessary, take a step back to create space between you and the attacking judge.	Use an exhibit, change positions in a grand way.
Emotion	Warm and engaging	Calm and firm.	Enthusiasm, energy.

	"I DON'T KNOW"	**SOFTBALL**	**GENUINE INQUIRY**
General	Admit you do not know, offer a solution, ask the judge for details or clarification.	Recognize it, deliver your short script notes on the issue, and help the court to write the order.	Teach and go deeper into the issue, use the judge's words to start.
Words	"I'm not familiar with that case." "I'm not sure, but I do know . . ." "That doesn't seem to be what we have here . . . ." "I was not aware of that." "I don't know, and . . . ." "I'm not familiar with that . . . ." "I'm unclear on the details . . . ." "That's not in the record . . ." "I'm not certain and don't want to say anything that is inaccurate." "I don't have that at my finger-tips. If you give me a moment, my colleague can provide that jump site . . . ."	"Absolutely, Your Honor." "That's precisely why it matters." "Yes, Your Honor . . . absolutely. I agree." "Yes, that's correct." "Yes, we see this the same way, Your Honor."	"I'd be happy to, Your Honor." "That brings us deeper into the issue of . . . ."
Voice	Projected volume, no upward inflection.	Calm, even pace. Stick with the rhythm. Stay in a slower paced rhythm to allow time to deliver your main points that align with the court.	Even volume. Measured, even pace. Keep range narrow.
Body	Broaden shoulder span. Do not collapse confident posture.	Warm, happy, pleased facial expression. Nodding during question (but not obnoxiously). Try taking a step back and give the floor to the judge. Bask in the agreement.	Minimize the size and scope to keep a humble posture. Keep listening, with facial expression relaxed or engaged, excited that you get the opportunity to share with the court.
Emotion	Avoid the look or sound of shock or surprise. Act matter of fact or dig in further to see if you can solve the judge's concern. Be more interested. Possibly ask the judge follow-up questions. Start a discussion.	Do not turn smug. When the judge is in your court, always be a gracious winner on that issue. If you gloat, the judge may flip. Share his concern instead of triumphing.	Portray patience instead of belittling the judge.

	HOSTILE QUESTIONS	**HYPOTHETICAL**	**MISINFORMED JUDGE**
General	First, try to hold your position. Try to reason with the court. Test the waters. Politely answer with your position. Do not wrestle; instead, disengage. If there is no movement from the bench, agree to disagree. Do not let the judge or opposing counsel shake you.	1) Confirm/clarify. 2) Answer *yes, no, maybe,* or *I don't know.* 3) Caveat—distinguish facts. 4) Transition—explain what you are asking for and not what you are not asking for. "But the result is different here because . . . ."	You must correct him, even when he confuses the facts/law in your favor.
Words	"May I move on?" "Sadly, we must agree to disagree on this point but we still win because . . ." "I'm so disappointed we don't agree on this point, Judge. May I move to my next point?" "It sounds like here we will have to agree to disagree, but I'm hoping you'll agree with me on [*move to next issue*]."	"As I understand it . . . ." "In your hypothetical, the facts are . . . ." "Yes, under those circumstances, the court would dismiss the matter . . . ." "It depends. In the facts of that situation . . . ." "No, Your Honor. That wouldn't change the decision." "One major difference with this scenario . . . ." "Your Honor, the court doesn't need to go that far. All we are asking for here is . . . ."	"Counsel is correct in this, but we win anyway because . . . ." "The holding in *X* was not . . . ." "To set the record straight, the facts here . . . ." "No, that's not the case here." "Those aren't the facts here." "That's not the applicable law in this case."
Voice	Slow pace, lower pitch.	Projected volume, no upward inflection. Increase pitch and range when you differentiate.	Projected volume, no upward inflection.
Body	Change palm position upward. Take a step back to avoid looking aggressive. Control facial expression while listening to reflect concern instead of annoyance.	Warm facial expression. Minimize gesture span. Try torso-hold home base to give the impression of listening intently to the judge's scenario.	Do not collapse confident posture.
Emotion	Reciprocate an aggressive tone with a welcoming emotion. Invite the court to continue speaking.	Have a sporting attitude about hypotheticals. They may help you reason with the judge. Your tone should be welcoming. Enjoy the intellectual exercise.	Return to your themes, so have an urgency to refocus the attention of the court.

	"WHY HAVEN'T YOU SETTLED?"	CONFUSED JUDGE QUESTION	"LET'S MAKE A DEAL" DISCUSSION
General	The judge is annoyed with both parties if he asks this question, so avoid being defensive or pointing fingers.	Recognize when the question is off the wall. Be patient with the court, bring back the bewildered judge.	The court is negotiating with counsel. Prepare for it ahead of time with your fallback position and what you and your client can live with.
Words	"We have tried to find a solution and may still but this motion presents a gating item to settlement." "We share your desire for a resolution, Your Honor. We're just not there yet." "A ruling in our favor today will help move the parties in that direction."	"Well, Your Honor, today's motion focuses on . . . ." "I understand your concern, but today we're here to . . . ."	"I can't go as far as you want, Your Honor, but I can . . . ." "I am having trouble with one aspect of your request . . . ." "I need to consult with my client to get approval."
Voice	Projected volume, no upward inflection. Possible to speed up with this answer to get back to your themes.	Slow pace, try lowering volume to sound more patient.	Projected volume, possible increase in speed if needed to return to theme.
Body	Nod head to show you want a solution as well.	Relax posture. Expand gestures to clearly explain substance.	Broaden shoulder span. Do not collapse confident posture.
Emotion	Avoid flippant or disrespectful attitudes.	Be validating, and lead the judge back.	Be helpful. Try to find a way to make a win-win.

	SUSPICIOUS JUDGE QUESTION	RABBIT HOLE	CONCESSIONS
General	Know ahead of time or through the course of the motion that the judge does not like or trust you or the client.	When a judge asks questions that stray you off your themes and often times into the weeds of the opposing counsel's unimportant counterarguments, it is necessary to back out of the rabbit hole and bring the court back to your main themes. Listen to the court's concerns, but do not feel compelled to follow the judge down an intellectual path that is ultimately irrelevant to the motion at hand. Affirm the concern and shift back to a major theme.	Get client's approval. Be careful of the long-term consequences. Think through the logical consequences of any concession. The judge may be asking a domino concession question: you give up one thing, and it necessary leads to the abandonment of several other things.
Words	No specific response. Here, you are managing your reaction. Keep to your talking points.	[*Answer quickly and directly, then lead him back to your points.*] "... but today we are here for the court to decide . . . ." "I share your concern with fairness, and right now the issue that faces us is ultimately about fairness." "That discussion sends us on a detour, which I'm happy to discuss for a moment."	*Can concede:* "Yes, Your Honor, my client can agree to that." "We're happy to stipulate to that decision, but we ask the Court . . . ." *Cannot concede:* "I have to talk to my client before we can agree to that." "Your Honor, that's not going to work in this situation." "We can't waive that, Your Honor."
Voice	Projected volume, no upward inflection. Slow down, lower pitch.	Projected volume, no upward inflection.	Brighten pitch and tone if you can stipulate.
Body	Longer eye-contact connection time. Broaden shoulder span. Use palm-up gestures.	Broaden shoulder span. Do not collapse confident posture.	Lean into conversation and be casual.
Emotion	Be careful. Do not exaggerate. Do not overestimate. Do not engage with the judge. Do not mirror his tone. Stay calm and professional.	Turn attitude. Be strong and lead the judge.	Be sincerely disappointed that you cannot concede, and be elated when you can.

CHAPTER SEVEN

STRUCTURE AND PREPARATION SYSTEMS

Motion hearings require flexibility. Situations change, judges change, adversaries change. Before entering the courtroom, you may have had a terrific plan to present your strongest argument, deal with your weakest, and win over the judge. Sadly, you were interrupted before you even had an opportunity to say your name. By the time the argument was over, you were stuck in a sinking whirlpool, not of your own making, but nevertheless one you were unable to escape. You never discussed your strengths. Your argument was hijacked. Good strategies exist to hedge disaster. You need to find the right techniques to succeed in this ever-shifting environment.

In this chapter, we discuss various preparation and organizational techniques to develop and deliver a successful motion. Some techniques should be a staple for all arguments; others depend on the skills of the advocate and the substance of the particular motion. To figure out what works for you, set aside enough time to try all the techniques. As you try a new preparation system, practice out loud and record yourself. Notice as you deliver whether the system of preparation 1) made things easier for you to have fluid thoughts and nimble responses, 2) became too cumbersome and hindered your ability to effectively deliver, or 3) provided an unsuccessful return. Keep track of which system works and which wastes your time. To successfully litigate, you must develop an individualized, efficient process that includes a combination of these techniques.

Just as every hearing is different, every advocate is different. Some attorneys struggle with questions, others with closing remarks, while others with remembering the details of case law. Your personal preparation system—a pattern of preparation that can be adjusted for a particular judge, motion, or opponent—should take into account your particular strengths and weaknesses. We start this chapter with the reliable parts and structure of most motion arguments, and end with a plethora of systems for you to use, either alone or in combination, to prepare for the uncertainties of a hearing.

7.1 Component Parts and Structure of Motions

Whether you are the movant or the respondent, your motions argument has a beginning, middle, and end.

7.1.1   The Beginning

The beginning constitutes the portion of the argument that the judge will remember most, so put your best material in this section. Think of the beginning as being so strong that it could stand alone and carry the day for you. Imagine the judge saying, "Counselor, I am short on time, so please limit your remarks to ninety seconds." A lot of ground has to be covered in the first opening section of your argument. Here is the list of four "must haves" in your beginning ninety seconds:

1) **Greet the court** ("Good morning, Your Honor. My name is John Doe, here representing *XYZ*.").

2) **State your theme and why it matters to the court.**

3) **Tell the court what you want** ("We ask the court . . . We are here today . . . Today we ask this court . . . ."). Be specific and simple in your request.

4) **Give a roadmap of what you wish to discuss in the hearing.** Because you will not be covering everything in your pleadings, tell the court where you wish to simply rest on your pleadings. Beginning your presentation with a roadmap follows the sound advice of speechwriters, who counsel to tell your audience where you are going, go there, and tell it where you have been.

> **Example**
>
> Good morning, Your Honor. My name is Daniel Smith, and I represent Mr. Sebastian. *Miranda* warnings are not merely suggestions from the courts. The police arrested Mr. Sebastian without Mirandizing him, and we ask this court to exclude the confession obtained during the arrest. This morning, I will discuss the *Miranda* standard and why the police failed to meet it.

7.1.2   The Middle

In the middle, discuss the facts of your case, the law, and apply the law to the facts in a way that supports your desired result.[1] Knowing how to structure the middle portion of the argument requires good judgment. The advocate needs to decide first *how* and *when* to present the facts and the law.

---

1. Chapters Four and Five gave pointers on handling the facts and law, all of which should be incorporated in the middle section of your argument.

To begin, decide whether 1) the facts and law are equally balanced between the movant and respondent, 2) the facts are predominantly on your side, or 3) the law is predominantly on your side. This classification helps develop the right structure for the middle of your presentation. When the facts and law are equally balanced, you can choose various organizations:

- **Issue-based organization**: blend the facts and the law together to cover a legal issue, weaving in the relevant facts. Move from one issue to another.

- **Sandwich approach**: develop the legal principle, present the facts, then finish with the law applied in the current situation.

- **Facts, principle, law**: present facts, then explain how the facts fit the public policy or legislative intent behind the law, which you cover last. This requires a patient judge or a law that is well-known to the court.

When the law is weak for you but the facts are in your favor, prepare an undisputed facts section and rely on the judge's sense of fairness to rule in your favor. When the law is on your side, lead with a simple presentation of the law and, if needed, use analogous fact patterns that prove your point and lead the judge away from the bad facts at hand. The tables below outline these various approaches to organizing the middle of your argument.

FACTS AND LAW EQUALLY BALANCED		
	Description	**Benefit**
Issue-based organization	Law and facts blended.	Useful to sequentially lay out one or more issues. Familiar pattern for judge accustomed to reading briefs.
Sandwich approach	Legal principle, facts presented, then law applied.	Less likely to be interrupted than if you begin with facts.
Facts, principle, law	Contextualized facts, public policy or legislative intent, law.	Use when there is law that everyone knows or that is court specific (discovery motions, preliminary injunctions).

FACTS ONLY ON YOUR SIDE		
	Description	**Benefit**
Through-line story	Facts-heavy delivery.	The equities of the case are highlighted rather than the law.

LAW ONLY ON YOUR SIDE		
	Description	**Benefit**
Leading with the law either through analogous case study or using facts of other cases	• Law and public policy • Facts • Three strongest points • Address anything damaging	Use when the law is on your side but the facts are not. Emphasis is on the law.

The middle is also the time to deal with your weaknesses. After you present your strongest arguments, tackle the other side's case. Generally, it is better to start with your strengths as opposed to defending your weaknesses, playing offense rather than defense. Do not begin your argument with, "My opponent says *X*, *Y*, and *Z*, but she is wrong." Rather, begin your argument with, "We win because . . . ."

The middle of the argument is where you should expect negotiations. Most judges wait for your ninety-second introduction and allow you to deliver a brief ending. The middle is when the judge usually digs into the motion. Answering her questions should be your first priority, as those questions highlight the obstacles between you and a favorable result. Questions often lead to a negotiation period, so include bargaining talking points and client-consented settlement points in your middle-section notes.

7.1.3   The End

The ending, much like your beginning, should have a structure and be kept brief—no more than two minutes. The ending is where you go when you see your time is over, when the court is clearly agreeing with you, or when the court asks you to "wrap it up." The ending should act like the final paragraph of a superb essay: it advances the original thesis. The finale is not just a repetition of the beginning; it pushes the argument one step further. It haunts the judge with a lingering thought by plunging directly into the judge's concerns. Because the argument may reveal a concern of the judge that you did not predict, develop the ability to nimbly adapt your ending. What you planned ahead of time may not end with the judge's top concern, so spontaneously react and edit the ending on the spot. That said, the "must-have" list for the ending includes:

1)   An appeal to the interest of the judge,

2)   A return to your theme, and

3)   "The ask," also known as the specific prayer for relief.

Consider this sample ending that appeals to the judge's concern for consistency while integrating the theme of limiting government's power:

> *Counsel*: The courts repeatedly stress the need for Mirandizing citizens under arrest. This keeps the government power in check. There is not confusion in case law about the exceptions, and the government does not assert a valid exception today. Your Honor has written extensively on the issue of *Miranda*. The police are well trained in how to issue proper *Miranda* warnings, and the police cannot pick and choose when they Mirandize a citizen under arrest. *Miranda* warnings are not merely suggestions from the courts. The police cannot ignore the courts' clear direction. We ask for the confession of Mr. Sebastian to be excluded from evidence because the police failed to provide even a basic *Miranda* warning to my client.

In a longer hearing, spend one minute appealing to the judge's concerns and interests. The lessons you learned in Chapter Two about discovering the interest of the judge are incorporated here in the ending. The concern may be a particularized concern with an issue in the case or a generalized concern motivated by the judge's interests, philosophy, or personality. Merge together the concerns of the court with your theme.

It is worth repeating that these appeals come only *after* your logical argument but *before* your ending, and are brief and focused. If you do not follow these rules, you risk the judge thinking you have nothing else to argue except fairness, resolution, or predictability. And choose one, maybe two, of these interests to appeal to and not all of them.

Merging your theme into the ending does not have to take a long time. Sometimes the ending should be short and sweet. An ending for the Humpty Dumpty case could be as short as the following: "Your Honor, this case is exactly like *State v. Jones*, and that's why the defendant deserves his day in court."

End with your prayer for relief and how to get there. Do not end with, "I want justice for my client!" or "If there are no further questions, I will sit down." End with a specific request for relief. "Judge, we ask that you deny my opponent's request for summary judgment and grant one for us because there are no material facts in dispute."

These last lines are your exit lines. They will be remembered. Prepare your last words ahead of time and practice delivering them. Stay connected to the judge through eye contact, and display a confident posture. Do not move to sit down until you have finished speaking. The conviction with which you deliver the lines just may be enough to convince the court that you must be right.

Exercise

Think about an upcoming motion hearing you have. Why is it fair for your client to win? Draft and deliver a one-minute argument on why the fair result is a ruling for your client.

Do the same appealing to the court's interest to clean his docket. Why would a ruling for your client lead to a quicker resolution of the case?

7.2 Think Flexibility

Thinking about a structure in a motion hearing is instructive, but oftentimes the structure is blown up by the circumstances of the argument. While it is generally advisable to deal with your weaknesses in the middle of your argument, if you are the respondent and the court seems to be buying one of the movant's strongest arguments, you cannot wait to respond. You must immediately tackle the adverse argument before the court will entertain your side of the case. On the other hand, if your opponent's argument is not capturing the court, then to begin with it only gives it credence. The line is subtle and can only be made by assessing, on the spot, the judge and the relative grip the argument has on him.

Other events can destroy your well-planned structure. Before the hearing, you may have thought that you had thirty minutes scheduled, but because the court is running behind, you have only five minutes. Your structure may disintegrate because the court begins asking you questions straightaway. You may not get your theme out, let alone a roadmap, before the first inquiry.

We now turn to a menu of preparation systems available to you to use alone, or in conjunction with one another, to help you remain flexible, yet persuasive and thorough, able to adapt to challenges you will face in court.

7.3   Long Script

Once you sketch your beginning, middle, and end, it is time to create a long script for the motion hearing. A long script has enough text within it to cover your entire allotted time. The long script is used to help you practice your entire presentation, and is eventually reduced into talking points for use during questions from the bench.

The long script will rarely be read to the court. The exception is motions where preserving the record is the only goal. Here, you deliver your long script only to lay the seeds for an appeal. Except for this and other rare circumstances, it is even dangerous to take your long script to the podium with you. The temptation is to read the script instead of delivering the argument in a confident, connected fashion. There are real dangers to reading or memorizing a text. Your voice will be flat, you will abandon non-verbal expression, and you will lose the connection to the judge. If you forget one word, you will crash because the memorized semantics will trip you. If you absolutely must bring your long script to the podium, take it with you, turn it upside down, and let it serve as a security blanket.

A good way to begin to draft your long script is to summarize your brief or your opponent's brief. Some advocates draft their long script as if they were putting everything on the record for an expected appeal. What would you need to say to lay the right foundation for appeal? The long script needs to be well-organized and efficiently written. If nerves completely paralyze you during questions, the written words of a long script can rescue you from the foggy brain or forgetfulness that strikes when adrenaline runs high. Remembering or referring to the section of the long script usually snaps an attorney out of the haze and allows him to reconnect with the judge.

A word of caution: there are stages of preparedness. The first stage is complete unpreparedness. Next, a basic framework of organization (often useful for attorneys who have fast-moving cases and rapid-fire motions with little prep time), then onto shaky memorization of phrasing and order, to a mastery of the substance, and finally to complete readiness, where you can add stylistic direction to your delivery.

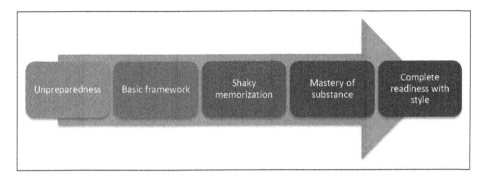

Complete readiness occurs when you have true control of the text—able to float in and out of it when necessary, yet you have spontaneity when needed to transition in and out of sections. Your delivery is natural and convincing. If you stop after the memorization phase, you will look robotic.

Take the example of an actor on stage. Once the actor memorizes the lines of a play or movie, he can appear robotic if he does not have complete mental mastery over the lines and is unable to focus on the delivery style. This balance of focus on the present moment and connecting with a listener while delivering substantive information happens in stages. Keep preparing through the memorization phase and you will appear natural and confident, able to deliver the finely crafted magic phrases that help win the day.

One way to break out of sounding mechanical is to practice phrasing your points in different ways. This allows you to test whether you are too locked in to the specific syntax in your long script. Should you need it, the long script is there to rescue you. But it should not be delivered as a stale, memorized piece to the judge. The hearing is supposed to be a discussion, an interaction, a chance to connect with the judge and find out whether he is, or is not, seeing it your way.

Example

Humpty Dumpty v. The King

Long Script for the King's Counsel: Seven-Minute Delivery Default Judgment Hearing

All people deserve their day in court, whether the litigant is a pauper or a king. [*Theme that resolves the suit and appeals to the judge's sense of fairness.*] Through no fault of his own, the King did not have his opportunity to be heard, and so we are asking you to set aside the default judgment that has been entered for Humpty Dumpty and against the King. [*The upfront ask.*] The King asks that the judgment be set aside because his counsel's failure to answer the complaint was the result of understandable excusable neglect, and he has a meritorious defense: Humpty Dumpty assumed the risk of his injury. [*Road map using magic words.*]

Humpty Dumpty climbed up on the wall surrounding the King's castle. [*Facts: pertinent facts only in a story fashion.*] We may never know why he did so, but we know that from his vantage point he was able to peer into the King's private chambers, where the Holy Grail was stored. The King's wall was an eight-foot brick wall, with rebar attached that formed a type of ladder. Mr. Dumpty climbed onto the makeshift ladder. From there, he had a great fall, and as we know, all the King's horses or men could not put Mr. Dumpty together again. Mr. Dumpty sued the King, timely serving him at the castle. One of the King's men promptly gave the summons to the Imperial Law Firm and attorney Emperor, who routinely represented the King.

Days later, the Emperor had a nervous breakdown. He was found on the street naked, but claiming he was wearing his new clothes.

The Emperor was so ill that he simply forgot to answer the complaint. Mr. Dumpty's attorney then sought default in the case. This court entered a default judgment, and two months later, the King's law firm moved to have the judgment set aside.

[*Intersection of facts and law, citing and distinguishing cases.*] The failure to timely respond to the complaint was excusable neglect on the part of the law firm. This case is very similar to the recent case of *Everystate v. Big Bad Wolf*. Everystate had filed a declaratory judgment action requesting the court find that Everystate's policy did not cover the intentional acts of the Big Bad Wolf in blowing down the home of the three little pigs. The Big Bad Wolf gave his summons to his law firm, Jack & Jill LLP, just as the King did here. It was the attorneys' illness—in that case, Jack fell down and broke his crown and Jill came tumbling after—that caused the default judgment. In *Everystate v. Big Bad Wolf*, our appellate court affirmed the trial court's order setting aside the judgment, as even the Big Bad Wolf deserved his day in court. Likewise, because it was not the King's conduct that caused the default, he should not be penalized for the acts of his law firm. Even the King deserves his day in court. [*Back to theme.*]

The King also has a meritorious defense. Mr. Dumpty assumed the risk when he climbed the wall, and therefore the King has no liability here. Assuming the risk is a complete defense to this lawsuit. The King will be denied the chance to assert that defense if this default judgment is not set aside.

[*Deal with your weaknesses.*] Now Mr. Dumpty's attorneys claim that the King does not have a meritorious defense. They claim that the wall is an attractive nuisance and this case is similar to *Old Witch v. Hansel and Gretel.* [*Distinguishing cases.*] It is not. In *Old Witch,* the attractive nuisance was a sugarcoated cottage dripping with icing, chocolate, and peppermint sticks that induced starving Hansel and Gretel into the home, where the old witch was able to confine them. But here, there was a brick wall that had metal bars embedded in it—a far cry from a candy-covered house. But, importantly, Your Honor, in *Old Witch,* even the old witch had an opportunity to have her day in court. The King deserves nothing less.

Our system of justice is premised on the concept that every person, a pauper or a king, big or small, young or old, should be given the opportunity to have their case heard by a fair and impartial judge or jury. [*Appeal to sense of justice.*] The King ought to have his day in court, just as Big Bad Wolf and old witch did. [*Theme.*]

There would be no prejudice to the plaintiff. While this case has been slowed down because of counsel's illness, we will agree to have the case fast-tracked to mitigate the delay. [*Negotiate with the court.*] It may be that a jury or a judge will ultimately find that the King is liable. But to deny him his day in court undermines confidence in the judicial process. The King deserves his opportunity for justice; he has done what he needed to do in order to be heard. His attorney dropped the ball, but that mistake should not result in this drastic denial of his right to a trial. He should not be punished for the actions of his attorney. He has a meritorious defense: that Mr. Dumpty assumed the risk of his own conduct.

[*The Ask.*] We ask that you set aside the default judgment, allow discovery to ensue, and set this matter for a pretrial conference. [*Specific request for relief.*]

7.4 Short Script

Once you have written your long script, you are ready to prepare your short script. The short script is a two- or three-minute speech concisely explaining why you win. It should begin with your theme, give the three strongest reasons why you win, and end with a specific prayer for relief. Use the short script when 1) you have only minutes to give your argument or 2) you have only limited time to set out your case between the questions of an inquisitive judge. The short script requires you to focus on what really matters.

To create your short script, take your long script section by section and decide how you would summarize each section. Also, highlight specific lines that can resonate with the judge and reverberate in his mind after you sit down—these will be your magic words. What is memorable about this section? What is critical to say? Can this section be dealt with in questions if the judge shows interest, but discarded altogether as part of the short script?

Example

Humpty Dumpty v. The King

Short Script for the King's Counsel: Three-Minute Delivery Default Judgment Hearing

> All people deserve their day in court, whether the litigant is a pauper or a King. The court should set aside the default judgment because the default was entered as a result of excusable neglect and the King has a meritorious defense.

> After Mr. Dumpty fell off the King's wall, he served the King with a complaint. The King immediately gave the complaint to his attorney. His attorney, the Emperor, was ill and was running around the kingdom without his clothes. The attorney was not in his right mind. It was because of the attorney's illness that Mr. Dumpty's complaint was not timely answered.

> The failure to timely answer the complaint was excusable.

> The King should not be punished for his attorney's illness.

The King, like everyone, deserves his day in court.

The facts of this case track the facts of *Everystate v. The Big Bad Wolf.* In *Big Bad Wolf*, the Wolf did not timely answer the complaint of Everystate because his attorneys were ill. The appellate court determined that the Wolf's failure to answer the complaint was excusable. Even Big Bad Wolf deserved his day in court.

Likewise, the King's failure to answer the complaint was excusable.

The King should not be punished for his attorney's illness.

The King, like Big Bad Wolf, deserves his day in court.

The King has a meritorious defense. Humpty Dumpty climbed on the King's wall of his own accord. It was Mr. Dumpty's actions that caused his own injury, not the King's. The King will prevail at trial. The King did not create an attractive nuisance. The wall was a clear sign notifying all to stay out of the King's grounds. This is unlike the case of *Old Witch v. Hansel and Gretel.* There, the old witch enticed the starving Hansel and Gretel with candy, while here, at best, the King's wall had a makeshift ladder made of rebar. In any event, whether an attractive nuisance is the cause of an injury is for a jury to decide.

And let me add that there is no harm to Humpty Dumpty if the court sets aside the default judgment. While this case has been slowed down because of the Emperor's illness, we will agree to have the case fast-tracked to mitigate the delay. Fairness requires the case be heard on the merits because:

> - There is excusable neglect.
> - The King should not be punished for his attorney's illness.
> - There is a meritorious defense.
> - The King deserves his day in court.
>
> We ask that you set aside the default judgment, allow discovery to ensue, and set this matter for a pretrial conference.

7.5 Bullet Points (with Transitions)

No matter what system you use, inevitably your notes should be turned into bullet points. The bullet points should be large enough for you to see at a quick glance. Make the font size at least 14 to 22 points. Usually, in the intensity of a hearing, you will not be able to read notes containing full sentences. If you need to search for your points on the page, your notes will be useless. The bullet points should have enough content to spark your memory on the broad topics you wish to cover, and on those smaller points that you always seem to forget. Each issue should have a separate page—one page, no more.

With their presentation organized and reduced to bullet points, most advocates find it easy to fill in the details of each point during the hearing. However, many advocates find the transitions between points more difficult. For seamlessly navigating between points, consider writing out your transitional phrases.

> **Example**
>
> ## *Humpty Dumpty v. The King*
>
> ## Bullet Point Outline
>
> ## Beginning
>
> All people deserve their day in court, whether the litigant is a pauper or a king. The court should set aside the default judgment because the default was entered as a result of excusable neglect and the King has a meritorious defense.

Rule 60(b), Excusable Neglect

Everystate v. Big Bad Wolf (Tab 1)

- Wolf's attorney ill
- Failure excusable
- Wolf deserved his day in court

The King's failure to answer the complaint was excusable

- King gave complaint to law firm (King Depo, p. 7)
- Emperor ill, did not answer (Court file 15409, p. 2)
- King should not be punished for his attorney's illness

Rule 60(b), Meritorious Defense

Dumpty assumed the risk (King's Man Depo, p. 3)

- *Jack and the Beanstalk v. Giant* (Tab 2)—adventurous boy, huge vine into sky, golden egg
- Dumpty scaled the wall (King's Man Depo, p. 3) (Tab 5)

Not an attractive nuisance

- *Old Witch v. Hansel and Gretel* (Tab 3)—peppermint, icing, candy, starving children
- Rebar, ladder, stone wall (Exhibit 17, picture of King's wall) (Tab 6)

> **Ending**
>
> - Fast-track offer?
> - Excusable neglect
> - Do not punish King for attorney's illness
> - Meritorious defense
> - King deserves day in court
>
> We ask that you set aside the default judgment, allow discovery to ensue, and set this matter for a pretrial conference.

7.6 Law-Driven System

For the law-intensive case, where the law is your strength, consider a law-centric preparation. It works well for those whose mind cannot hold and remember the specifics of each case and law. Use the law-driven preparation system for the judge who is an expert in the area of law and is known to be an active questioner.

For each issue, create a separate page that summarizes the cases, statutes, or rules relevant to that issue. Too much information will be difficult to access during the heat of the argument. Instead, provide just enough information to remind you of each cite. For cases, your notes should look like this:

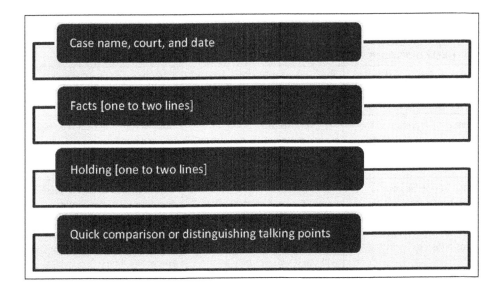

For statutes and rules, this format should be helpful:

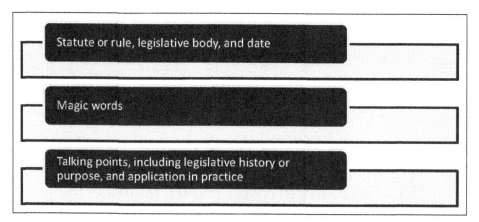

At the back of your three-ring binder, make separate tabs for each case, rule, or statute so you can access the details easily. If you would rather use a folder system, either electronic or paper, create a separate folder for each authority. Chances are that you will never reach for the full case or statute, but having them near you will give you confidence.

7.7 Question-Driven System

For those who fear questions, anticipate them and plan your answers. Formulate transitions back to your main points. Bullet-point the likely questions in the first column, the answers in the second column, and your transitions in the third column. Again, your main notes should not be over three pages and the questions should be separated by issue.

Rule 60(b), Excusable Neglect		
LIKELY QUESTIONS	**ANSWERS**	**TRANSITIONS**
Why couldn't another attorney in the Imperial Law Firm handle this?	"Because of the intimate relationship between the King and the Emperor."	"The illness of the Emperor should not damage the King's opportunity to be heard."
Doesn't Everystate v. The Big Bad Wolf *completely resolve the case?*	"Yes, it absolutely does, Your Honor. It stands for the proposition that everyone deserves his day in court."	"Just as the King deserves his day in court . . . ."
You did not file your request to set aside the default judgment until two months after the judgment was entered?	"Yes, we did, Your Honor. If you would take a look at the file stamp on the judgment and then look at the file stamp on the motion to set it aside, you will see it was actually a little less than two months."	"I have copies of those two documents, if you would like me to approach. (Tab 7) The King acted promptly; he should not be punished for the Emperor's illness."

7.8 Point/Counterpoint

Identify your opponent's main arguments. Reduce them to a few words, listed on the left side of a page. On the right side, bullet-point your response to her argument. Again, each issue should have its own separate page. As you listen to your opponent, you can highlight those points made and cross off those not covered.

HUMPTY'S ARGUMENTS	RESPONSE
There is no meritorious defense, because there was an attractive nuisance.	*Old Witch v. Hansel and Gretel*—peppermint, icing, candy, starving children (Tab 3). Rebar, ladder, stone wall (Exhibit 17, picture of King's wall) (Tab 6).
Dumpty could not have predicted the severity of his injuries.	Dumpty scaled the wall (King's Man Depo, p. 3) (Tab 5). Dumpty is an egg (Dumpty's Depo, p. 5) (Tab 8).

7.9 Theme

Write out your themes and sub-themes for each issue. Write out a variety of ways to say each theme so you do not sound scripted and you keep the interest of the judge. After every question or main thought, go back to your theme or its variation. This serves as a bold reminder to constantly transition back to a winning theme.

> **Example**
>
> ***Humpty Dumpty v. The King***
>
> **There is excusable neglect.**
>
> - The failure to timely answer the complaint was excusable.
> - The King's failure to answer the complaint was excusable.
>
> **There is a meritorious defense.**
>
> - Humpty Dumpty climbed the wall on his own accord.
> - The King will ultimately prevail on the merits.
>
> **The King deserves his day in court.**
>
> - If the Big Bad Wolf deserved his day in court, certainly the King does.
> - The King should not be punished for his attorney's illness.

7.10 Deliver It from Your Hand

This system is for the attorney who does not have much time to prepare. Here, the attorney has three to five points that he wants to make and uses his fingers to remember the points. Find three to five points you wish to make. Boil them down to one-word reminders. Then deliver them, in order, without notes. Keep points crisp and in logical place so you can recall them. For example, Saint Teresa of Calcutta gave the "Gospel on Five Fingers." She would say the words, "You did it to Me," as she held up each finger of her hand. She explained:

You—who was responsible

did—that action was necessary

it—what they needed to do (feed the hungry, give water to the thirsty, visit those in prison, shelter the homeless, visit the sick)

to—that the actions are in service of another

Me—why and to whom, God

Humpty Dumpty v. The King could be reduced to "RISKY":

Risk—Humpty's actions were risky

Illness—the emperor's illness and excusable neglect

Same—the law should treat all the same

King—how he was served and what he did with the complaint

Yucky—wall of brick with rebar, no attractive nuisance

Likewise, for a motion with limited preparation time, you may wish to cue yourself with easy-to-remember prompts.

Exercise

Take a case that you have argued, or will, and reduce it to a three- to five-word phrase. Practice arguing, using each word as a cue.

7.11 Logistics

All these note systems, except long and short scripts, may be laid out side by side on the podium or counsel table. You may keep a binder on the podium with your long or short script, as long as it is not too bulky. If it is, tuck it on the shelf inside the podium, or keep it with your co-counsel. It is not advisable to use a laptop for your notes. The screen is a physical barrier between you and the judge that will affect your connection to the judge. In many courtrooms, you must present behind a podium and a computer hides even more of you, creating yet another obstacle to bonding with the court. Tablets laid flat work.

The following table shows advantages and disadvantages of all the different preparation options discussed in this chapter.

PREPARATION SYSTEMS		
System	*Advantages*	*Disadvantages*
Long script	Confidence building, clarifies thinking. Keeps an advocate who has trouble with word-smithing (too long winded or not detailed enough) on the right track. Tends to calm nerves. Used for the disengaged judge.	Tough to take to the podium with you. Risk that you will fall into reading to the judge. Less eye contact. Not able to connect with judge or watch his reactions. If memorized, the tendency is to be flustered when one word or phrase is missed. Bound by words on page. Stifles expression in body language and flattens vocal delivery. Tends to create overall fast or slow delivery. Quickly sounds stale.
Short script	Clarifies thinking to be concise and to the point. Simplifies difficult concepts. Develops magic phrases. Keeps attention of the court. Takes less time. Useful for rebuttal later. Easier to manipulate style changes than the long script. No fear of not making a record.	If memorized, can be delivered flat with no connection to the court. Tendency to be flustered when one word or phrase is lost. Risk of the advocate knowing too much and starting the story in the middle.
Bullet points (with or without transitions)	Security blanket for things you always forget. Helps with organization when law and facts are merged in deliveries. Easier to talk more conversationally off bullet points than full script. Transitions give you confidence. Magic phrases are front and center.	If too detailed, not easy to see and you cannot find your points quickly enough. You can get lost in the paper. May have to shuffle multiple pages. Usually flattens gesture pattern because hands are needed to keep place on outline and mark what has been covered.
Law driven	For the law-heavy case, the case law and statutes are at your fingertips. Use when the judge is an expert in an area and wants to get into specifics. Gives you confidence that you will not forget the facts, holdings, or principles of multiple cases.	If judge is a big-picture person, then case-by-case analysis is too specific. If too detailed, difficult to use in the argument.

PREPARATION SYSTEMS		
System	*Advantages*	*Disadvantages*
Question driven	For those nervous with the prospect of answering questions. Plan transitions from questions back to your strengths. Use with an active bench.	If the judge does not ask any questions, you have wasted your time.
Point/counter-point	Able to quickly respond to your opponent's arguments. Works well for rebuttal arguments. During your opponent's argument, you can cross off those points not covered.	You have a danger of becoming too defensive and may not offensively argue your case.
Theme	Keeps you focused on your main arguments.	Lacks detail. You lose the specifics.
The hand (three to five points, cued by words within a short phrase)	To be used when there is minimal preparation time. Allows for focused and simple directed delivery. Perfect for the spontaneous discussion with the judge. Easy to remember for you and the judge. This allows for the fullest expression of your vocal instrument and your body language because there are no notes. It fosters a relationship with the judge, as if you were discussing it outside the courtroom.	Lacks detail. You may forget something crucial for the motion. It is not right for a complex motion or the judge who wants to discuss the specifics.

CHAPTER EIGHT

REBUTTALS

Rebuttals are risky. Done well, they serve as a way to briefly address your opponent's arguments and remind the court why it should find in your favor. Done poorly, they bore and frustrate the judge and could turn the court against you. Often, an advocate would have been better off abandoning the rebuttal all together. Think strategically about when a rebuttal is the right move. If the court chews up your opponent's arguments and clearly sees things your way, resist the temptation to deliver a rebuttal. That is right: pass on a rebuttal. Stay seated. If the court or opposing counsel misunderstands law or facts, use the rebuttal to quickly set the record straight. Even if the correction cuts against you, you gain long-term credibility. If you feel like your ship is sinking, go directly to the damaged hull and address it. If it is clear that the damage is irreparable, this is the time to suggest or open negotiations to avoid drowning.

There are certain types of rebuttals that should never be spoken.

- **Laundry list or checklist deliveries.** Here, the attorney stands up and lists all the arguments, grievances, and counters in a checklist format. Because a listener can only remember a few points at a time in oral delivery, the laundry list has little impact and is remembered as a waste of time.

- **Same old song replay.** Argument regurgitation is an ineffective way to connect with the court. Many judges dislike rebuttals for this reason. The court hears one side, then another—and the rebuttal ends up being nothing more than a rehash of one or both. If you have delivered a memorable and full motion, a repeat is unnecessary. When the attorney uses the rebuttal to deliver the motion again, it is usually the same order and wording. Instead, treat a rebuttal like a good essay ending. Finish with a twist or development on the main theme. Offering the court a way to see things from a different angle is often useful, as opposed to sounding like a broken record repeating the same thing.

- **Defensive whining.** When a rebuttal is used to complain about opposing counsel or his arguments, a judge will shut down. To a judge, a defensive and whiny rebuttal sounds weak and annoying. Imagine hearing two children tattling on one other. Instead, address points without complaining. Show strength.

- **Smugness.** If the judge dislikes opposing counsel's reply to your argument, there is no reason to stand up and use rebuttal time to rub it in her face. Instead, be dignified and unemotional, and do not crow over your opponent's apparent loss.

- **My way or the highway.** Oftentimes an attorney delivers a rebuttal without addressing issues that clearly needed to be covered. Even worse, not addressing your opponent's argument looks conceited. This will not gain you favor with the court. If the judge seems perplexed or needs information or to be brought back to your side on an issue, address it head-on. Do not treat the rebuttal as if you ignored your opponent and the judge as they discussed the motion. Listen and respond accordingly.

There are times when a judge is interested in or confused about an aspect of the argument. Often, your opponent made a point, and the rebuttal gives you a chance to convince the judge that your position should prevail. When the right rebuttal moment presents itself, be prepared ahead of time. A successful rebuttal delivery requires preparation, but also flexibility and quick decisions. Because judges are impatient with rebuttals, *keep them short.* Unless the judge wants to keep talking, keep rebuttals to no more than five minutes, even in a long hearing. To prepare for a successful rebuttal, divide the rebuttal time into three parts.

REBUTTAL		
First	**Second**	**Third**
Respond directly to the judge or opposing counsel	Make corrections, clear up misunderstandings in fact or law	Go to the heart of the judge, write the order

8.1 Part One of Your Rebuttal (Two to Three Minutes)

To successfully plan for the first portion of the rebuttal, think of this section as being on the defensive. It should last for only two or three minutes, and should directly address a couple points where your adversary did the most damage to you. These points can be predicted ahead of time. The predetermined simple points for this section will rein you in and prevent a laundry list from leaving your mouth. Read the judge—his questions and reactions will let you know where you have to go and how much work you have to do to bring him back to your side. Deal with the problems first and get them out of the way before you go back to what you want to talk about.

The topics and talking points can be outlined ahead of time, with high predictability. Simply create bullet points that summarize the opposing counsel's predictable arguments, with corresponding rebuttal talking points. If you research the judge, you may be able to predict his areas of concern. Listen closely during the opposing counsel's actual argument, and respond directly with the help of your pre-scripted responses.

Although you have thought ahead about your response, do not be tied to your script. Weave the judge's words into your rebuttal. Doing so will let the judge know that you listened to his concerns, while at the same time you can use his words to align yourself with him and lead him to your view.

There are a couple of ways to organize this first section of your rebuttal. One way is to reorganize the framework and redefine the issue. In a motion for summary judgment, your opponent may seem to have made points with the court on three factual issues in dispute. You may argue in response that these factual matters do not matter. What matters is the law that applies. In other words, change the framework.

Another way to reply is to argue a few key points that are determinative of the case. This is usually the section where advocates feel tempted to throw in a laundry list of "gotcha" points. When following this approach, be choosy and respond to a couple of the hot items discussed by the judge and opposing counsel. If you have prepared a topic list, with responses on one page in front of you at counsel's table, you can listen closely and expand any necessary talking points.

The following example was prepared as the rebuttal to a large, multidistrict litigation (MDL) motion in the Seventh Circuit by Mariah Brandt, a partner at Pillsbury, Winthrop, Shaw, Pittman LLP. The MDL is a class-action products liability suit.

To set the stage for you: opposing counsel just sat down after calling Acme's motions petty, whiny, and hyper-technical. They attempted to shift class parties without leave of court.

> *Brandt*: Your Honor, nothing Acme has raised is technical or petty. Properly crafted claims—standing, jurisdiction—these are foundational issues. Plaintiffs call these things mere procedures. Well, procedures keep things fair and create fair dealing.
>
> Adding Smith and his California subclass creates problems. They don't even know where he belongs. They don't know which court will welcome Smith and his subclass once this MDL is finished. We can't even properly address the jurisdictional issues until we know what action he is in.
>
> And the *manner* in which Smith and the subclass were added, without any leave of court, creates a dangerous precedent.

8.2 Part Two of Your Rebuttal (One Minute)

The second part of the rebuttal is optional, and covers sub-themes or less predictable topics covered by your opponent. "Less predictable" means that you can anticipate many possible things but cannot exactly determine which sub-themes will dominate the discussion. Some advocates make the added mistake of furiously taking notes to capture opposing counsel's position and the judge's response. This technique usually results in a less thoughtful and more disorganized rebuttal. Instead, prepare a manageable list of predictable sub-topics with a planned, thoughtful response.

Use the second part of the rebuttal to set the record straight on any misunderstandings or misstatements heard during opposing counsel's argument. This second part should be eliminated if nothing needs to be corrected. The judge's patience is running thin at this point, so avoid correcting a misstatement that will not make a difference in the end. For example, if opposing counsel states that the contract was signed on February 2 when the correct date is February 3, with no meaningful events in between, let it go. Additionally, avoid making distinctions without a difference. For instance, it is best not to stand up and correct opposing counsel's word choice— your client "slapped," not "smacked," the victim, as an example.

Correct an interpretation of the facts or law that makes a difference to the case. This could be when you discover during opposing counsel's argument that the judge is confused on a higher court's position on the pivotal law in the case. That is worth correcting, even if the truth cuts against your present win. You can use transitional language like, "Your Honor, let me correct the record . . . . Just to be clear, in the facts here . . . ."

A key emotional goal here is to stay intellectual and avoid correcting opposing counsel in an accusatory fashion, as if you caught him. You want to remain courteous and to extend opposing counsel the benefit of the doubt. The judge will determine if the opposing counsel misspoke or lied. Instead, just state the correction and allow the judge to dig in with any questions that may arise. Also, the judge may directly ask opposing counsel to chime in with a response to the correction, so this could become a true discussion. Be willing to stand back from the podium for a moment to allow opposing counsel to respond to a judge's direct question to him. Avoid talking over opposing counsel or increasing your volume in an attempt to overpower him. The point of this second part is to set the record straight on matters of facts or law.

To prepare for this second section of the rebuttal, comb through the reply brief and collect any inconsistencies, misstatements, or misrepresentations of facts or law. Have this list at counsel's table in a Rebuttal Checklist, and quickly check or highlight anything that must be addressed after hearing the discussion between opposing counsel and the judge.

Here is an example of a pre-planned Rebuttal Checklist used during the same MDL hearing, when listening to opposing counsel's argument. It is a predicted summary of opposing counsel's best arguments. As opposing counsel delivered, Mariah Brandt could watch the judge's reaction, check the two to three items that deserved attention, and address those items during Part Two of her rebuttal.

REBUTTAL CHECKLIST

- ☑ The court has subject matter jurisdiction because all of the plaintiffs have suffered an injury-in-fact as a result of the Acme products.

- ☐ Smith should not be struck because it is not necessary to seek leave of court.

- ☐ The subclass claims should not be dismissed because notice is not required.

- ☑ Several plaintiffs have standing to pursue a claim.

- ☑ The plaintiffs have standing to seek injunctive relief.

- ☐ The plaintiffs' claims are valid.

And here we have sample rebuttal language for Part Two:

On the face of the complaint, all of the claims fail because the plaintiffs have not alleged the correct business relationship with Acme. And they will not be able to, because Acme does not sell directly to consumers. The plaintiffs even concede this point.

Not only do all the plaintiffs fail to state a claim, we now know that the plaintiffs do not even have standing, based on their sworn deposition testimony. While the plaintiffs urge this court to ignore this fact, the bell cannot be un-rung.

This same exposing deposition testimony reveals that there is no imminent threat of future harm and that all plaintiffs have an adequate remedy at law. The Supreme Court mandates that injunctive relief be denied.

If it is clear, after the first two parts of rebuttal, that the judge is not buying what you are selling, now is the time to turn to your Plan B. You will hear the judge's resistance in his argumentative or sarcastic tone. You will see his resistance in his skeptical face.

Plan B is the fallback position that you have agreed to with your client before the hearing. It may be that you have no fallback, because losing this motion does not matter in the long run or you believe that you have a good chance of a reversal on appeal. But if you do have fallback, now is the time to begin the negotiations. Suggest that the court does not need to go as far as you or the opponent asked him to go. Recommend a middle position. Appeal to the "inner Solomon" of your judge.

8.3 Part Three of Your Rebuttal (One to Two Minutes)

Part Three returns you to the offensive. You have done the hard work of getting the judge back to the middle; now is the time to talk about what you want to talk about. Go to your strongest point as to why you win, but say it in a way that you have never said it before.

Your goal is to leave the judge with a deeper understanding or reason to rule for you. Often, the last gem is the public policy argument. For example, if you are asking for a default judgment to be set aside, now is the time to talk about the reasons the law prefers a decision on the merits. Tell the court that resolving a case on the merits enhances the credibility of our judicial system, while procedural maneuvering has the opposite effect.

Provided that you did not include an appeal to the interests of the judge in your opening argument, you may choose to place it in the end of the rebuttal. In any event, end by returning to your theme and your specific request for relief. Continuing on with our Acme example from above, consider this rebuttal delivery:

> The complaint is flawed. Not only does it fail to state certain claims, fail to show jurisdiction, and fail to show standing, but it includes the claim of unjust enrichment, which does not even exist in California law.
>
> It is the epitome of judicial efficiency for this Court to determine these issues now.
>
> This Court should grant Acme's motion to strike and dismiss in its entirety.

Whether you are about to deliver the beginning, middle, end, or rebuttal portion of your argument, knowing *how* to deliver it makes all the difference. Now that you have powerful substance well at hand, Chapter Nine provides presentation techniques to persuade the judge on the stylistic front.

CHAPTER NINE

"NOW THAT I KNOW WHAT TO SAY, HOW DO I SAY IT?"

Psychological research reveals how important the style of your delivery is to your message. Psychologist Albert Mehrabian's research[1] reveals that audiences understand oral communication in the following manner:

- **Vocal**—38 percent through voice quality
- **Visual**—55 percent through body language and appearance
- **Verbal**—7 percent through the message

These percentages shed light on just how important the delivery is for any oral communication. Too many attorneys focus solely on the content in a motion hearing and neglect the style of delivery. The judge should have received the bulk of the content through the papers. The hearing allows you to utilize the visual, vocal, and emotional components Dr. Mehrabian notes to persuade the judge. When you are speaking, you want to reach a point of mastery over the substance so you can focus on your stylistic delivery.

The goal of oral communication training is to give you skills that, coupled with your expertise and experience, will help you explain a complex matter or persuade even the most difficult judge of the legitimacy of your position. Fine-tuned oral communication skills help you craft arguments that appeal to the widest possible variety of judges without sacrificing your individuality. In motion hearings, certain behaviors, mannerisms, and styles can offend, while others appeal to most judges. Advocates should shed the habits and inclinations that do not appeal, and develop the appropriate successful techniques.

Some attorneys naturally perform stylistically better than others. Some attorneys have the gift of a great voice. Some attorneys put you at ease or inspire you simply with their body language. Some advocates win an argument because of their emotional mastery over a substantively difficult motion. If you are one of these individuals, you

---

1. Mehrabian, Albert. ""Silent Messages"—A Wealth of Information about Nonverbal Communication (Body Language)". *Personality & Emotion Tests & Software: Psychological Books & Articles of Popular Interest* (Los Angeles, CA: self-published, 2009) (retrieved Apr. 6, 2010).

can become even more successful by training and developing your gifts. If you are not naturally gifted, you can learn techniques that improve your skills.

To improve the stylistic delivery at a motion hearing, your goals should be to:

- Identify and ditch bad habits,

- Cultivate good habits so you can employ them at their peak level, and

- Enhance those good habits at which you already excel.

9.1 Voice

Ultimately, you want a friendly, engaging, clear vocal quality that can be heard by the judge. You will use variation of volume, speed, pitch, range, and word stress to create interest for the judge. The variation should be a blend of natural variation and purposeful variation implanted for emphasis.

A judge connects to the quality or tone of the attorney's voice. Your aim should be to display your instrument's best quality by properly using volume, articulation, pitch, inflection, speed, and pauses. As your voice improves, you will learn its limitations and can work on techniques to compensate for those limitations. This is important to your professional advancement, and you will achieve results by paying steady attention to each element.

9.1.1 Volume

Project your voice enough for the judge to hear you clearly. The amount of projection needed changes depending on courtroom acoustics and size. In general, project more than you think is necessary. A judge and a court reporter should not strain to hear you. The audience cannot comprehend what it cannot hear. It is far easier to tone down the volume if you notice the judge reacting poorly to your loud volume. That will likely not be the problem. Most of the time, volume problems happen because attorneys do not project enough. When the judge or the court reporter asks you to speak up, overcorrect.

Divide volume into two categories: projection and focus. Project enough voice or sound to create the right decibel level necessary for the courtroom. The steadier and stronger the flow of air from your lungs, the greater the decibels. To be heard, you also need to focus your voice toward the back wall behind the judge.

Often, when attorneys consult their notes too much, volume vacillates because the sound is not consistently focused in the same direction. A noticeable volume change happens when he looks up from the page and then speaks a line. The judge hears two different volumes because the attorney is delivering the words in two different directions. This volume vacillation is often accentuated with a podium microphone. If he turns his head toward the microphone, volume increases. If he looks away, volume decreases.

To correct volume vacillation with a microphone, do not rely on it to project your voice. If you rely on the microphone, you are likely to lean into the podium, placing your mouth too close to the microphone. This is hard to recover from—if you try to adjust and align your posture, now the judge cannot hear you. That leaves you hunched over and kissing the microphone.

9.1.2   Articulation

Another barrier to clear comprehension for the judge is the lack of good articulation. An advocate must pronounce the words. Crisp consonants frame the vowel sounds, making them—and you—more confident and expressive. In contrast, when you mumble, the essential sound elements of the words glide together, and you appear shy, unconfident, and wavering. Enunciate clearly with crisp consonants. Practice aloud tricky words, especially names.

A note about accents: Accents should stay intact, unless they impede the judge's ability to understand you. Clearly articulating the consonants will keep your accent in check.

9.1.3   Pitch

Singers classify themselves by voice part—soprano, mezzo, alto, baritone, and bass. To keep it simple, classify yourself as having a voice that is generally high pitched, medium pitched, or low pitched. You should speak in the middle of your register. Good projection often raises the overall vocal pitch of certain speakers. If your voice creeps too high and you notice it, lower it slightly.

For the most part, judges prefer lower-pitched speaking voices, unless a voice is of such excellent quality that they are drawn to listen to it. A high-pitched voice usually sounds whiny, shrieking, piercing, and diminutive.

Women generally have higher-pitched voices. Careful attention must be paid to overemphasizing words with a high-pitch stress. Men often speak in a low-pitched voice, subconsciously dropping into an even lower-pitched voice to sound more masculine and authoritative. The trouble with low-pitched voices is two-fold: they are harder to hear and can easily slip into a monotone drone.

9.1.4   Range

Range means the span of high to low notes you use when speaking. Once you know your own habitual pitch (generally high, medium, or low), begin noticing whether you cover a wide range of pitches in the course of a conversation or monologue. Actors use a wide range of notes—the wider the range, the more expressive a speaker sounds. A robot's "voice" would have a narrow range of notes, leaving it virtually monotone. If you find yourself bored or tired when listening to someone speak, they are probably displaying a narrow vocal range. This boring mode of speech dampens the audience's attention. A good attorney speaks with a wide range of pitches, accentuating his voice with high and low pitches as the moment demands. This pitch variation keeps the attention of the judge and helps communicate emotion.

Stretching your vocal range allows you to express emotion when you are making your presentation and helps keep the judge's interest. You may find that you have a wider vocal range when standing, because most speakers take advantage of better breathing and posture in a standing position—it gives them the ability to reach higher and lower notes in their voice.

9.1.5   *Inflection*

Your voice should naturally stretch to different pitches, covering a range of notes. An attorney creates patterns of speech depending on when he causes his voice to fall in pitch at the end of clauses, phrases, and sentences. Imagine a "bossy voice," full of deflections in pitch at the end of each phrase. This voice barks a command with every descent in pitch. Now imagine someone who sounds insecure and uncertain about his position, questioning each phrase with an upward turn in pitch. In America, some call this repetitive pattern a "Valley girl" voice, "upspeak," or "upward inflection."

Properly used, *upward inflection* is the occasional upward tick in pitch, at the end of questions or to keep attention in the midst of a series. It is imperative that you have the proper inflection and vocal descent to your voice when you end a declarative statement. There are several good reasons to raise your pitch at the end of a phrase:

1)   To ask a question, even rhetorical.

2)   In a series ("We requested emails, photographs, and copies of the contract." The voice should inflect in pitch at "emails" and "photographs," telling the listener that the series or list is not finished yet. The voice should fall in pitch at "contract," signaling to the judge that the series is complete.).

3)   Before the conjunction of a compound sentence ("Mrs. Smith assaulted her neighbor, and her boyfriend fled the scene." The voice should inflect in pitch on "neighbor.").

4)   For specific emphasis. Every speaking rule has exceptions. There are times when we purposely raise the pitch of the final syllable or word in a declarative sentence to signal irony or curiosity or frustration. ("Surely, the legislature did not intend that.")

Countless attorneys cannot properly inflect and descend in pitch. Sadly, improper upward inflection becomes a pattern for many speakers, even in court. Once it becomes a pattern, the voice lacks confidence and sounds insecure or patronizing.

Improper patterns of inflection can be corrected by properly stressing operative words. Operative words are words stressed or accentuated to convey meaning. When you speak, you "make points" by stressing operative words. Say the following sentence out loud: "Judge, Washington Bank will close the deal in October." Your voice determines the operative words in the sentence for the listener. If timing is important, you would stress the word *October*. Say the sentence with that word stressed. If the finality of the deal is important, you could stress *close the deal*. Stressed words become the "operative words" in any sentence.

For your voice to inflect confidently, inflect it up somewhere in a sentence so your voice can descend in pitch at the end of the sentence. To drop the tentative upward inflection pattern, train your voice to inflect on operative words within the sentence. This process of breaking an irregular speech pattern takes time and practice.

9.1.6   Speed

Speed is where advanced advocacy takes flight. Crafting the pace of your delivery is essential to success, but balancing the fast and slow segments is an art. You can learn how to shape the piece by using speed. There are several guideposts to speed that every attorney should know:

- Judges dislike super-slow speakers. First, she gets bored. Second, she feels like you are being condescending when the pace is too slow.

- Judges often get lost with fast speakers. If your pace is too fast, the judge is turned off. The rate of speech must be delivered at a digestible pace for messages to flow into the judge's mind. You also run the risk of sounding over-rehearsed and robotic.

- Increasing your speed in a list or series makes it sound like you would have more facts to list if time permitted. If you have a chance to list a series of facts in your favor, speeding through them makes the judge think there are endless examples waiting in the wings. Slowly defining things makes them sound singular and finite.

9.1.7   Pauses

Pausing equals power. Imagine being in a courtroom with a judge who speaks like a scared rabbit, covering time with needless fillers such as *uh, eh, ah*. Now imagine a different judge, who projects confidence with silent moments. Pausing makes the listener wait for the speaker. It allows absorption time for the information just given. Pausing also cushions those words the attorney wants remembered. Pausing is essential.

Pauses are powerful in a motion hearing. They allow the judge to hear a higher degree of complexity because the attorney allows her to catch up. There should be natural breath breaks within any spoken delivery. In a breath mark, the attorney refuels the voice effortlessly for the next section of spoken text. Pauses can also be strategically positioned. Here are a few places where short pauses should be strategically placed:

1) After you greet the court ("Good morning, Your Honor.");

2) After you state your name;

3) Between sections to transition;

4) Before answering a question; and

5) To set up a meaningful phrase or word.

9.2 Body Language

Body language, used in concert with your well-crafted message and voice, is a powerful persuasion tool. Nonverbal communication includes your stance when delivering or seated posture at counsel's table. Body language nonverbally communicates feeling and meaning. Body language areas covered in this book include home bases, gestures, facial expression, and eye contact.

Your posture, gestures, and facial animation should match the energy level of your message. Your body should appear connected to your words. The judge wants to pay attention, so do not be the speaker that makes her struggle to stay interested. Most of us know an acquaintance who acts so subdued in social situations that you wonder if they need an oxygen infusion to show some life. Keeping life injected into your delivery becomes easier when you focus on body language.

As you notice problems and set goals to correct, avoid telling yourself to simply stop the offending body language behavior. Instead, give yourself something better to do in its place. To improve body language, *replace* ineffective motion, posture, or activity instead of eliminating it. For example, if you want to stop randomly pacing back and forth, *replace* the pacing with deliberate movement at key moments at the hearing. If you want to stop an overused repetitive gesture, *replace* the gesture with specifically chosen and timed alternatives. If you want to correct an awkward brooding expression, *replace* it with an appropriate cheerful one.

We come in all shapes and sizes, with different energy levels and a variety of backgrounds. Because of this diversity, strive to feel natural in a way that is suitable for the courtroom. Here, body language needs to be professional, respectful, and polished while being yourself.

Improving body language can be hard to change for some advocates. Presenting a more confident appearance may feel fake or out of your comfort zone. Find the courage to stretch your comfort zone and you will see results. Research such as Amy Cuddy's inquiry into body language and the "power pose," which has been popularized by her well-known TED Talk,[2] proves that being more confident on the outside makes you actually more confident on the inside.

9.2.1 *"Home Base"*

Still positions taken between gestures are "home bases." Every attorney should find a few standing and seated home base positions. Actor's neutral (hands resting straight down on either side) and a torso hold (hands connecting at a height between belly button and belt) are staples. The others depend on your personality and body shape. A tall, imposing man may want to try a one hand in pocket home base during a discussion with the judge. A smaller-framed woman needs an elbows-wide, shoulders-back podium hold to look commanding in a courtroom.

A home base is a calm posture from which gestures flow, allowing you to show passion and confidence. Start noticing your own home bases when you speak to friends and family. Once you find solid home bases when standing and seated, practice transitioning in and out of each home base, eventually gesturing in and between these positions.

For shorter hearings, you may notice that you only need one home base. If you plan on speaking for an extended time, a few home bases help break up the presentation for the judge and keep your body energized for the duration. Remember that audiences need a change approximately every three minutes. Sometimes a presentation will not have logical three-minute breaks in substance, but you can reset the judge's attention by changing your home base.

Moving from base to base prevents you from looking like a statue. Below are some home bases that you should try while you read this book. You may have already incorporated some into your presentation style. Others may feel strange until you try them out. You may find that you already have a better one that suits your personality. If so, use it.

---

2. Amy Cuddy's TED talk, *Your Body Language Shapes Who You Are*, may be viewed at https://www. ted.com/talks/amy_cuddy_your_body_language_shapes_who_you_are?language=en (last visited Aug. 19, 2016).

MOTION HOME BASES	
Hands resting on either side of a podium	This is formal. Have no tension in hands—do not grip the podium. Avoid looking like you are holding on for balance.
Actor's neutral	Keep body aligned, arms at side, chest lifted. Good position to reach after you have incorporated yourself into the arguments.
Hand in pocket	Personality and body-frame driven. It is generally more useful for men, because women's slacks rarely have pant pockets. This home base can purposely be used to make you more approachable. Do not play with anything in your pocket, and use only one hand.
Hands clasped at mid-torso	Rest hands just below rib cage. Do not clasp with tension. Keep arms relaxed.
Hand holding a prop	The prop can be a writing utensil or remote clicker/pointer. Be careful not to play with the prop or point it at the judge.
Standing to the side of a podium or table, with one hand resting on it	This is effective for a question and answer session, and/or to break up the monotony of a podium position. Some judges allow you to use this home base if you are passing documents or visuals to the bench and opposing counsel. Others allow this as long as you are close enough to touch the podium.

The home bases need to be decided beforehand, so you know how you will stand and command the space during the hearing. Because most presentations occur behind a podium, the home base options discussed here should be used at a podium.

Your available space at a podium is larger than you think. Imagine a triangle formation, with the tip of the triangle at the top of the podium, and the base of the triangle spanning behind you two to three feet. This is how much space you have to use in a motion hearing.

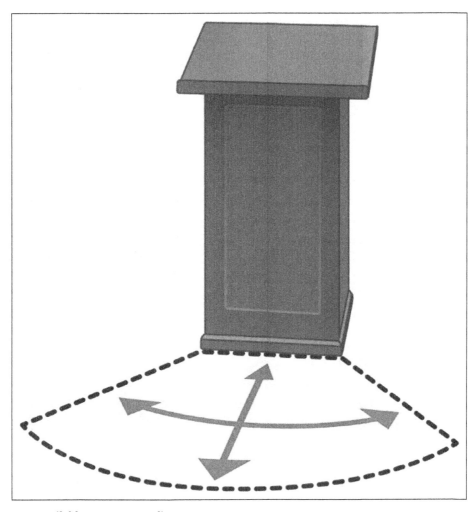

Your available space at a podium.

There are certain physical behaviors that should not be done at court. While there are a few exceptions to these prohibitions, do not try these in court:

- **Wonder Woman**—two hands on hips in a resting pose
- **Point**—Hand gesture with pointer finger flexed forward at the judge or opposing counsel
- **Military rest**—hands behind back
- **Fig leaf**—hands clasped below beltline
- **Choir boy**—hands clasped at bust level

- **Podium avoidance**—it is not electrical, it will not shock you, interact with it at some point
- **Podium lean**—avoid lounging on and lunging at the podium

Do not confuse changing home bases with distracting movements during the hearing. Swaying, rocking, and pacing should be avoided. Some advocates who rock back and forth find that placing feet slightly "pigeon toed" helps stabilize them. For attorneys who sway side to side, place one foot slightly in front of the other to prevent this frustrating movement.

Exercise

Stand up in front of a mirror. Do all the bad habits listed above, one at a time. Say goodbye to those positions. Now, find three comfortable home bases from the table provided, and practice moving in and out of all three.

9.2.2   *Gestures*

Your gestures should be fluid in court. They should match your message and intensity. They should, above all, match your personality. Gestures are a powerful tool, allowing you to bring the judge's attention to key points, move the plot forward, and leave the court with a memorable impression. Gestures also help advocates remember text. To memorize long presentations, add gestures and blocking (directions for the speaker where to move and stand) to help sear the performance in your mind.

Gestures should be connected to the words. Imagine a bad actor trying to perform Shakespeare, throwing out random gestures a half-second behind the lines to be illustrated. This disconnected style is uncomfortable to watch and signals that the attorney is fearful or inexperienced.

What gestures should you use? Those that are productive and varied. Observe your natural gesticulation pattern. Notice what kinds of emphasis gestures you use, when you use them, and how wide they span in space. In a hearing, vary your gestures so they stay fresh and move the argument forward. If a judge remembers a repeated gesture (karate chopping the podium, wagging a pointed finger), you need to vary those movements. If the judge sees movements that help describe the text, the judge will understand better and remember more.

Gestures help bring the judge into the conversation. Everyone has a natural gesture size, frequency, and style. This is the natural emphasis-gesture pattern that an advocate should know to determine how many gestures should be added or removed from your repertoire. A skilled advocate adds to their natural gesticulation pattern. To create a visual imprint in the judge's mind, a smart attorney uses the space in front of him to connect gestures with the substance of the delivery. There are natural and easy ways to connect gestures to the meaning.

- **Chronological**. When describing a timeline of events to the judge, use your hands to show the timeline and when certain events occurred. Keep the placement consistent. The rim of the podium offers a perfect sightline for the judge to see a horizontal timeline. This physical display of elapsed time can be a powerful way to show the court the impact of time. For example, if you are waiting for interrogatories, *showing* the judge how long you have waited while you tell her can make a huge impact.

  Tip: Show the past dates to your right, so the judge across from you sees the past on her left and the future on her right.

- **Compare and contrast**. When describing two different positions or courses of action, you can divide the space in front of you into two pieces. One position receives gestures placed on the left side, and the other position receives gestures placed on the right side.

  Tip: Once you set up a regime in space (the defendant's position discussed on the right, the plaintiff's on the left), keep all related gestures in the correct zone.

- **Enumeration**. When describing a short list of things, number the items both verbally and physically. You can number points on your hands or use the space in front of you.

  Tip: Try showing a foundational enumeration by starting low with a gesture, and showing each additional number at a higher level physically with your gestures.

Much has been written about the psychological effect of using gestures with palms facing down and gestures with palms facing up. In general, use palm-up gestures when you offer a suggestion to the court and ask for agreement. Use palm-down gestures when describing something that is not in dispute, something in the past, or something that has been decided.

Gestures signal your level of emotional control. Keep gestures smooth and completed in court. An attorney should avoid rapid-fire gestures, flailing gestures, or the huge or tiny gesture that looks out of place. Complete a gesture, and return to your home base.

9.2.3 Facial Expression

More and more research shows that there are core universal facial expressions. Using the right facial expressions can be your most subtle and powerful way to convince a judge. Knowing how intensely you express emotion on your face will help you recognize when you need to tone down expression and when you need to amplify expression.

Resting Facial Expression: How to Find and Change It

Everyone has a resting facial expression. Some people maintain a grin on their face when they are not talking or reacting to a speaker. Others maintain a perplexed look. Some settle into an aggressive expression. An attorney's resting facial expression gives the judge a first impression of the advocate. Video-recording yourself in presentation and listening modes will help you find your resting facial expression. A good friend or colleague can also shed light on your resting facial expression, so ask him.

Once detected, decide if it should be controlled or changed. If so, pick a pleasant expression and continually remind your facial muscles to return to this newly identified pleasant expression. With enough muscular training, those facial muscles will respond to your newly picked resting facial expression when you speak to the judge.

Matching Facial Expression with Your Words

When you utter certain words and phrases, the facial expression needs to match the words spoken. Lead the judge with your facial expression. Do not mirror hers. Your facial expression will direct the judge towards the right empathetic reaction. If you say, "My client is a respected member of his community," then you should have a proud expression on your face. If you say, "This injunction will ruin my client's business," then you should have a concerned expression on your face.

Poker Face and More

There are times when you need to hide emotion in a hearing. The judge or opposing counsel can be truly trying. Things do not always go your way. Training your facial muscles to have a pleasant "poker face" is required to hide offensive emotions (anger, smugness, conceit, defensiveness) and/or defeat and weakness. To hide emotion, it is important to control not only your facial muscles, but your vocal tone and body language.

When a certain offensive emotion begins to creep into your psyche:

- Regulate your breath by taking even and effortless breaths,

- Avoid hitting high-pitch notes in your voice, and

- Keep your speed even—speaking too slowly can sound patronizing and/or seething mad and speaking too fast can make you sound defensive, angry, or scared.

9.3 Make Genuine Eye Contact

Eye contact is powerful and moving. The judge senses when you actually look into her eyes and when you cheat, looking near or above her eyes. Keep eye contact with the judge until you complete a phrase, point, or section. Think about eye contact as a way to ensure you have explained yourself, and that the judge understands you. Glean information about your own messaging by the way the judge listens.

Eye contact needs to be handled sensitively. In general, keep eye contact with the judge 70 percent of the time. Hold eye contact with the judge for three to four seconds, or the completion of a thought. Give the judge breaks in eye contact by training yourself to look at notes or down and away instead of glancing up. If you stare too long at the judge, you run the risk of crossing into an uncomfortable zone. Instead, allow one another to look away, think, or let the judge take notes.

Sometimes, the judge is the one who avoids eye contact. If you cannot get the eye contact of the judge, make sure you are projecting your voice in her direction, change home base, and keep looking at the judge as if she is listening (the law clerk is probably watching).

Refining the physical performance end of your courtroom advocacy technique can be, in the beginning, overwhelming and feel a bit forced. Start slowly: choose just one stylistic habit at a time to replace or enhance. It may be awkward at first, but with repetition, these practices will soon become your new normal and feel natural. To inspire your development, take every opportunity you get to watch outstanding advocates whose courtroom performances you admire. The magnetic qualities these advocates possess combine into something we call the "It Factor," a topic we discuss in the next chapter.

CHAPTER TEN

THE "IT FACTOR"

You know what to say, how to prepare, and how to deliver your argument. All these things being equal, certain attorneys still rise to the top. They are just better. We trust them. We like them. We want to listen to them. The final ingredient needed to succeed is the "It Factor." This is what separates good attorneys from great attorneys. The It Factor can be broken down into conviction, confidence, likability, and stage presence. Here is how you develop that special something.

10.1 Conviction: Believe in Your Cause

Those who show conviction for their clients' causes move judges. Let the judge know that you believe in your argument. To show conviction:

1) Deliver a confident introduction of yourself;

2) Ask the court for relief within the first ninety seconds;

3) Use a theme that allows you to show enthusiasm for your cause;

4) Keep eye contact with the court;

5) Project your voice so you can be clearly heard;

6) Deliver your sentences with a descent in pitch at the last syllable of the phrase, and stress the right syllables with passion; and

7) Stand tall and limit your movement, communicating with your body that you are strong in your stance.

Judges gain the resolve to rule in your favor from you. If you do not believe in your case, neither will the judge. Show you have confidence in your position; your enthusiasm will be contagious.

Conviction in the righteousness of your cause does not mean rabid zealotry. Do not appeal merely to the emotions of the case. Neither must you discount summarily the other side's argument as if it is so weak it does not deserve your attention. After arguing your strengths, consider the other side's position—and then crush it with logic.

Judges connect with the technically imperfect argument from the passionate, albeit clumsy, attorney more than the silky-smooth, technically perfect attorney.

10.2 Confidence: Conquer Your Nerves

Most people lose confidence when nerves attack. A large part of appearing confident is controlling the nerves. The stress of arguing a motion is real and crippling at times. Adrenaline rushes generally spike during the first minute of any public-speaking event. That minute is charged with adrenaline. The adrenaline gives the speaker energy and natural presence, but it can also be visibly inhibiting. A motion hearing is full of high-stakes nerves. The judge will naturally feel sorry for the advocate who has severe hand shaking, or forgets all the words in his head and is dumbstruck. But this is not the sympathy we want as advocates. We do not want the judge to feel sorry for us. We want to persuade the judge to rule in our favor.

Each advocate should discover her personal, psychosomatic reactions to nerves, then find a technique to control, mask, and, at times, combat it. Most of us need to focus on controlling these "nervous tells" for the first sixty seconds of an adrenaline rush. Certainly, nervous tells can creep into a presentation midstream, but most advocates can sense this happening and control it.

The ending of a presentation is different. Many attorneys reach the end of their presentation and begin a relentless attack of self-doubt. To finish quickly, the attorney ends up throwing away the impact of the ending, rushes through the final remarks, and quickly sits down. The techniques listed below in the table should be used for the nerves that hit at the beginning, but also at the end if the editor in your mind hinders your ability to finish strong. Once you know your nervous tells, you can overcome them with proper techniques.

Most attorneys have a place where their tension resides. Many contract their jaw muscles or hands, for example. Record yourself giving your ninety-second beginning and look for your tension areas. Once you identify them, work on relaxing those areas when you speak. If you notice that you hold tension in your jaw, massage your jaw joint and facial muscles before presenting. If your hands show nerves, stretch them before and during a communication. Use a video-recorder to see if this works. Keep "air between your fingers" as you gesture, so your hands look relaxed. This will also help prevent you from wringing your hands, if that is your tic. Another trick to release hand tension is to contract the hand muscles in a fist, then release the tension. Doing this "tense and release" technique moments before beginning the hearing can channel adrenaline and release the nerves building in that area. You can also use this tense and release exercise for your jaw and face by scrunching your facial muscles, then relaxing. (Best to do this in the courthouse bathroom away from opposing counsel and your client.)

The following table describes many typical nervous responses, and offers advice to overcome them.

IDENTIFYING AND IMPROVING NERVOUS TELLS	
PROBLEM	**SOLUTION**
Tightening of throat at the top of the neck and back of the mouth	*Long term*: Practice singing fast-paced songs with low-high skips and repeatedly stretch the back of the mouth and top of the throat with a closed-mouth and a deep yawn. *Short term:* As you stand to deliver the argument, tip your chin and yawn with your mouth closed to stretch out your throat and release tension in those muscles. Start with a slightly lower pitch.
Racing heartbeat	*Long term*: Practice breath regulation exercises and audible, deep "sighs." *Short term:* On the day of the hearing, slow down to a methodical, slow saunter using deep breaths. When nerves start, exhale on a loud, audible sigh (in private). As you stand to deliver the argument, sigh silently as you approach the podium, have a glass of water at the edge of counsel's table ready if needed, breath regularly with easy inhalation (do not take huge, deep breaths). Take an extra moment to settle yourself and your notes at the podium.
Nausea	Eat a low-acidic meal and consult your doctor for anti-acid medications, if needed.
Posture collapse	*Long term*: Practice strengthening your overall posture and stance so a habit of good alignment is formed. Stand against a wall. *Short term*: Pick a starting "home base" beforehand, and practice your beginning at that home base every time you rehearse the argument.
Upward inflection and increased filler pattern	Highlight the operative words in each phrase, but avoid choosing the last word in any sentence. Practice voice pitch inflection at each highlighted operative word. Audio-record the first minute of your presentation, checking for upward inflection. Re-record until the right amount of stress is put on the highlighted operative words.
Shaking hands	Flex opposite muscle groups (if your hands begin to shake, flex muscles in your legs or buttocks). Start the hearing by holding a prop (pen or eyeglasses). Choose a starting home base that rests your hands on either side of the podium. Do a finger-tension exercise (stretch fingers out and hold tension, then quickly release; repeat).
Quivering voice	If you hear the quiver, slightly lower pitch and increase volume. As you stand to deliver your argument, tip your chin and yawn with your mouth closed to stretch out throat and release tension in those muscles.

| IDENTIFYING AND IMPROVING NERVOUS TELLS ||
PROBLEM	*SOLUTION*
Sweating face	In the morning before the hearing, apply a clear, mattifying, sweatproof primer makeup.
Foggy brain and/or forgetfulness	Memorize the first and last five lines cold, until you can do it in your sleep. Consider memorizing transitional lines between sections.
Loss of breath control	Before you stand up, tip your head down and yawn with your mouth closed to open the throat muscles that control the voice box. When approaching the podium, use silent sighs to rush breath out. Between questions, take a short pause before answering. Effortlessly inhale before answering any question. Train yourself to inhale and immediately speak instead of holding breath at the top of the phrase. Find a triangle within the podium space to shift foot position.
Supersonic speed	*Long term*: Use a metronome or a metronome application on a smartphone (such as Pro Metronome) to regulate your rehearsal vocal speed at 155 beats per minute (*allegrissimo*, at 4:1 on the metronome setting). *Short term:* Be a slave to punctuation. At all commas and periods, take a silent pause.
Filler words (*um, ah, er, and, so*)	*Long term:* Train yourself to compress your thumb and forefinger on one hand every time you reach a punctuation mark. As you gently squeeze your fingers, it should cue you to take a breath that replaces the filler. Through repetition, you create a physical cue to link the inhalation with the pause at the punctuation. *Short term:* Be a slave to punctuation. At all commas and periods, take a silent pause.
Unnecessary movement	If you rock back and forth, place feet slightly "pigeon toed." If you sway side to side, place one foot slightly in front of the other to prevent this frustrating movement.
Fidgeting (hair flipping, wardrobe adjustments, pen clicking, coin jingling)	Use a prop to focus your nervous energy. Plan specific gestures that you synchronize with pre-chosen words. Write these in the margins of your notes. Any physical distractions (long hair in face, pocket full of coins) should be controlled. Empty your pockets.
Eyes that drift/roll up and out	Train yourself to look down (almost pretending to consult notes). Sweep eyes down to your page, capture a line of text, reconnect with the judge, and deliver the text.

10.3 Likability

Pathos includes the ever-important "likability" factor. In the competitive legal arena, most attorneys have the legal acumen and proper level of experience to adequately, and perhaps superlatively, provide legal services. Yet clients gravitate to the attorney they like to work with—those with a good "deskside" manner. The likability factor is critical for success in a motion hearing.

The smartest attorney is not always the best attorney. Having brains does not mean you are a good communicator, and being brilliant does not guarantee success. To be successful in a motion hearing, attorneys need to communicate with power and feeling. Emotions and attorneys are not always the best of friends—finding the right pathos is an afterthought for some attorneys. In the appropriate situation, however, the right dose of emotion can often win the day over a well-reasoned, but stiffly presented, argument. Learning to act expands your ability to express the right emotion. Where appropriate, your smart choice during a hearing could be an appeal to humanity, a gesture of friendship, an empathetic tone, a frustrated expression, or a brusque challenge.

Still, some attorneys are proudly offended at the idea of an attorney acting. In reality, however, we all act. In most day-to-day activities, we pretend when we behave a certain way or hide our true emotion. When a senior partner or client asked you to attend a function at 6:00 a.m., you pretended you did not mind and you smiled during the function. You were acting. When the judge berated you in a packed courtroom for interrupting a witness, you took a deep breath and responded civilly. You were acting. When the client decided to take her business in a different direction that materially changed the agreements you had worked on for months, you pretended to not mind. You were acting. The fact is that attorneys who have a reputation for being "hard to work with" often lack the desire or skills needed to act. They do not play nice. They force their instinctive emotion on the rest of their team instead of responding with reserved emotion or civility. You already act—so let's talk about enhancing your techniques so you can be more persuasive when doing so.

To deliver the right emotion, you must be perceptive enough to sense the emotional needs of the judge. You know the moment is right in your gut. Acting trains you to display that emotion—through the words you say, your voice, your body language, or your posture.

Before you weave the right emotions into a hearing, you need a firm foundation to support your credibility. For an attorney, this foundation is likability. Any emotion you portray is built on likability. If you fail to establish a certain rapport with the judge, you run the risk of being seen as a fake, a charlatan. Judges like positive, honest, confident, generous attorneys. Civility does not just sound nice—it helps increase your overall likability with the court. Once the judge likes you, it is harder for him to rule against you. He may still rule against you, but you want to make him think twice about doing it.

No matter what the case, there is always a moment in your greeting to the judge to be warm and engaging. This does not mean you need to be oozing with friendliness or flattery. It means you look professional, energized, and grateful to have the time with the judge.

"Toast the Judge" Exercise

The ultimate goal of "Toast the Judge" is to improve your tone in court as well as represent your client professionally in an oral presentation. A good way to start is to take a friendly toast and convert it to an introduction in a formal arena. Imagine yourself at a wedding reception or a banquet. You have been asked to raise a glass and give a toast to the judge. This toast should start by giving a brief background of how you know the judge, and then continue with the reasons why you enjoy practicing law in his courtroom. Here is an example:

> Judge Steve Apple and I met at a charity event in Los Angeles ten years ago when he first started practicing law. Since then, he has been elected to the bench, and serves the community.

Now keep the same emotional tone you used to make the social toast above and change the text to the opening of a hearing in court. Here is an example:

> Your Honor, my name is Barbara Frank, for the Department of Justice. My client seeks summary judgment.

Practice varying your tone until you reach the perfect attitude for the specific presentation at hand. Practice in the extreme, since your nerves will shrink the progress you made in the actual performance.

The likable attorney balances defending his client with respectfully dealing with his opponent. This takes an enormous amount of self-control and a constant effort to tell the court you are giving the other side the benefit of the doubt despite bad behavior. Here are specific tips to incorporate into your demeanor.

1) **Avoid extreme or offensive emotions, conclusions, or positions.** You already know to avoid hyperbole, but avoid casting offensive labels or positions at all. What not to do: "Your Honor, he is lying!" A better choice: "Your Honor, his statement today contradicts his statement yesterday."

2) **Avoid smugness, conceit, and sarcasm.** Acting like a snob, bragging about your greatness, and finding flaws in another will rarely

increase likability. What not to do: "Your Honor, give me a break. She is clearly such a novice." A better choice: "Your Honor, I'd like to take a step back. Opposing counsel missed the deadline, but we will stipulate to a reasonable extension."

3) **Do not self-deprecate.** Self-deprecation from an intelligent, successful attorney usually comes across as false humility. Instead, heartily laugh at yourself when you actually fall on your face. Mistakes are not always terrible. Honest stumbles sometimes provide you the chance to pause and restabilize, a chance to laugh at yourself, a chance to show the court that you are human. What not to do: "I am not a smart enough attorney to stand up here and unpack the terms of this agreement." A better choice: "This is a complicated provision that is difficult to follow."

4) **If you overstate or misspeak, immediately correct your mistake and own it.** Even if time has elapsed during your argument, stop and address the mistake. What not to do: "I will not concede that point. I said it, Your Honor, and I meant it." A better choice: "Your Honor, I misspoke earlier. I stated that the tolling period was for four years. I misspoke. I should have said two years."

5) **Chivalrously deal with your opponent.** Rules of engagement: no interruptions, insults, sour facial expressions, scoffs, or verbal attacks. What not to do: "Your Honor, opposing counsel is a scoundrel of the worst kind." A better choice: "Your Honor, opposing counsel replied to the interrogatories only after six months of reminders."

10.4 Stage Presence

Some people have the charisma that pulls all eyes to them. What makes certain people stand out in a crowd and be remembered? There are certain common threads in attorneys who naturally possess stage presence. Most of these threads can be woven into your own style.

1) **Display excellent posture and energy to command the courtroom.**

2) **Use fluid, natural gestures.** When your gestures are small and choppy, your erratic flails overcome your poise.

3) **Dress the part.** Just as actors have costumes, your attire is a tool to use. If you wear flashy or immodest clothing, the judge pays attention to your attire instead of you. If you dress slovenly or disheveled, judges do not take you seriously—or worse, could be offended at the disrespectful attire. If your dress is professional, attractive, and tailored, you look the part of a successful attorney.

4) **Be adaptable and quick on your feet.** When something goes wrong in a presentation—and something always goes wrong—attorneys with charisma bounce back, recover, and move on. When you blunder a word, quickly correct it without embarrassment.

5) **Sincerely connect with and care about the judge.** A charismatic advocate communicates effectively by invoking empathy. You do not necessarily need to feel the emotion you describe, but you have to help the judge feel that emotion. Build a relationship with the judge by staying present in the moment.

6) **Keep your emotions in check.** When actors perform on stage, they transmit emotions across a wide space in an auditorium to the audience. When an actor acts in a movie, the emotional changes are more subtle and understated because the camera is often at close range. An attorney delivering a motion argument should be somewhat in between, like a film actor, showing emotional subtleties, not exaggerated emotional displays intended to reach the folks in the third balcony. You are hired to think reasonably. Your emotions must be reasonably displayed. Avoid the extremes—weakness, bossiness, abrasiveness, and hysterics.

7) **Transition smoothly between emotions.** When you try new emotions and inject acting techniques into your presentation, concentrate on the transitions from one emotion to another. Most attorneys fail to make smooth transitions to the next emotion (e.g., moving from the friendly greeting to the serious tone needed to deliver the theme in the next section). When you practice delivering your argument, rehearse the transitions. If you can smooth these out, the argument will flow with proper pathos. Use the words of your transitional phrase to change from one emotion to another by delivering the transitions with a matter-of-fact tone. Use the transition line as a blank slate between two differently toned sections.

10.5 Conclusion

Most importantly, you must be genuine. This requires that you know your personality and transmit it sincerely to the judge. A judge can smell a fake from a mile away, so be yourself. Be true to who you are.

You will never improve without a healthy dose of humility. You must constantly ask for feedback and welcome critique. Watch expert advocates and incorporate the winning techniques that mesh with your style. You have strengths and weaknesses, and you will spend your career fortifying what works for you and improving your skills.

You can only do this with practice. Find every opportunity to rehearse in a courtroom, before a mirror, or with a friend. There is no substitute for practicing aloud. Experiment—mimic the techniques of great attorneys. Adjust and refine until you find your unique style. Practice may never make you perfect, but it will make you better.

Appendix

This Appendix contains a blank Motion Planning Worksheet, which was discussed in Chapter One at 1.12.

To download this Worksheet and customize it for your own use in motion practice, please visit our download center at the website below and enter the password at the prompt.

http://bit.ly/1P20Jea

Password: PWM1

MOTION PLANNING WORKSHEET	
Legal Elements	**Statute, Cases, Law**
Critical Good Facts	**Bad Facts**

Theme and Sub-Themes		

Time Allotted	**When**	**Where**
Witnesses	**Subpoenaed Date**	**Exhibits**

Questions	**Responses**

Strongest Argument
Argument 2
Argument 3
Opponent's Argument 1 and Response
Opponent's Argument 2 and Response
Opponent's Argument 3 and Response

Fallback Position	**Client's Approval**

Index

A

ARGUMENTS (*See* **PREPARATION FOR HEARING**)

B

BODY LANGUAGE
Generally, 9.2
Facial expression, 9.2.3
Gestures, 9.2.2
"Home base" 9.2.1
The law, 5.9

C

COURTROOM (*See* **JUDGE**)

E

EXHIBITS AND DEMONSTRATIVES
Considering, 1.8
Facts, 4.9

EYE CONTACT
Genuine, making, 9.3

F

FACTS
Bad, 4.6
Conclusions, not, 4.2
Context before, 4.1
Coulda, woulda, shoulda, 4.3
Crucial, only, 4.4
Exhibits, 4.9
Overstating, 4.7
Reasonable inferences, 4.5
Speed crafting, 4.12
Story of your motion, creating, 4.11
Visual pictures, creating, 4.10
Word choice, 4.8

FACTUAL THEORY
Review and refine your, 1.2

I

"IT FACTOR"
Generally, 10.5
Confidence: conquer your nerves, 10.2
Conviction: believe in your cause, 10.1
Likability, 10.3
Nervous tells, identifying and improving, 10.2
Stage presence, 10.4

J

JUDGE
Alignment with opposing counsel or you, 2.4.2
Confused, 6.3.9
Conservative versus liberal views, 2.3.2
Consistency in rulings, desire for, 2.1.4
Courtroom and
    Generally, 2.5
    Humor, 2.5.2
    Informal versus formal, 2.5.1
    Law clerk, 2.5.4
    Overworked motions-call, 2.5.3
    Questioning, extent of judge's, 2.5.5
Disengaged judge, engaging, 6.3.14
Docket, overloaded, 2.1.3
Elected or appointed, 2.4.1
Expertise in area of law, 2.2.2
Fairness and justice, 2.1.1
Hostile question and insistent judge, 6.3.6
Humor, 2.5.2
Judicial philosophy, 2.3.1
Knowledge - sliding scale
    Generally, 2.2
    Expertise in area of law, 2.2.2
    Reading nothing, little, or everything, 2.2.1
Law clerk, 2.5.4
Law to, reading, 5.9
Misinformed, 6.3.10
Motivating concerns, his
    Generally, 2.1

National Institute for Trial Advocacy

Q

R

S

SCRIPT
> Long, 7.3
> Preparing, 1.13
> Short, 7.4

STRUCTURE OF MOTIONS
> Beginning, the, 7.1.1
> Bullet points (with transitions) 7.5
> End, the, 7.1.3
> Fingers to deliver, use your, 7.10
> Logistics, 7.11
> Middle, the, 7.1.2
> Point/counterpoint, 7.8
> Script
>> Long, 7.3
>> Short, 7.4
> Theme, 7.9
> Think flexibility, 7.2

T

THE LAW
> Body language, 5.9
> Dealing with, techniques for, 5.1
> Discussing conversationally, practicing, 5.7
> Know, 5.3
> Oversimplify, do not, 5.2
> Pitfalls, identifying, 5.8
> Practice aloud, 5.6
> Purpose of or common sense reason behind, arguing, 5.5
> Reading to judge, 5.9
> Simple, keeping it, 5.1

> Stylistic switch, flipping, 5.8
> Use elegantly, 5.4
> Verbal signaling, 5.9
> Vocal change, 5.9

THEMES
> Common motions, 3.3
> Creating your, 1.3
> How, the, 3.3
> Structure of motions, 7.9
> Techniques, 3.3
> Using your, 3.4
> What, the, 3.1
> Why, the, 3.2

TIME OF DAY
> Motion, effect on your, 1.4

V

VOICE
> Generally, 9.1
> Articulation, 9.1.2
> Inflection, 9.1.5
> Pauses, 9.1.7
> Pitch, 9.1.3
> Range, 9.1.4
> Speed, 9.1.6
> The law, vocal change, 5.9
> Volume, 9.1.1

W

WITNESSES
> Calling, considering, 1.7